P9-BYG-241

ALSO BY PICO IYER

Abandon

The Global Soul

Tropical Classical

Cuba and the Night

Falling Off the Map

The Lady and the Monk

Video Night in Kathmandu

SUN AFTER DARK

SUN
AFTER
DARK

FLIGHTS INTO
THE FOREIGN

Pico
Iyer

Alfred A. Knopf
New York
2004

This Is a Borzoi Book
Published by Alfred A. Knopf

Copyright © 2004 by Pico Iyer
All rights reserved under International and
Pan-American Copyright Conventions. Published
in the United States by Alfred A. Knopf, a division
of Random House, Inc., New York, and
simultaneously in Canada by Random House of
Canada Limited, Toronto. Distributed by Random
House, Inc., New York.
www.randomhouse.com
Knopf, Borzoi Books, and the colophon are
registered trademarks of Random House, Inc.

Portions of this work originally appeared,
often in very different form, in the following:
*The American Scholar, Buzz, Condé Nast Traveler,
Harper's,* the *New York Review of Books,*
the *New York Times Book Review,* and *Time.*

Excerpts from *When We Were Orphans* by Kazuo Ishiguro
reprinted courtesy of Alfred A. Knopf, a division
of Random House, Inc.

Library of Congress Cataloging-in-Publication Data
Iyer, Pico.
Sun after dark : Flights into the foreign / Pico
Iyer — 1st ed.
p. cm.
ISBN 0-375-41506-8
1. Iyer, Pico—Travel. 2. Voyages and travels. I. Title.
G465.195 2004
910.4—dc21   2003054612

Manufactured in the United States of America
First Edition

In San Francisco it has long been dark. It is nearly 10 at night there. Here, endless sun. I have done everything. Sleep. Prayers. And I finished Hesse's *Siddhartha*. Nothing changes the endless sunlight. And in this light the stewardesses come with questionnaires that we must all fill in. Why do we travel?, etc.

—Thomas Merton, flying, in October 1968, to Asia (a journey from which he would not return)

Contents

SUN AFTER DARK

THE
PLACE
ACROSS
THE
MOUNTAINS

One midsummer evening in La Paz, just before New Year's Eve, I went out into the dark to find a taxi to take me to the modern suburbs. I hadn't slept—or not slept—for many days, it seemed, and so, not quite myself, I hailed a cab and told the driver to take me to a Mexican restaurant I had read about, down in the warm valley to the south. We followed the curves of a mountain road, and came very soon to a darkened grid of long, straight streets, stretching in every direction. I repeated the address of the place to the driver, but Indian names are hard to make out for a foreigner, and soon, very soon, we were lost.

Security guards watched us from their posts, outside the villas of the rich; every last detail seemed picked out in the lunar quiet. Up above, in the commotion of the Indian area, everything was a swarm of color; here the streets were laid out as precisely as if with a ruler and pencil. We turned one way, turned another, and on every side were faced with long, straight streets, concluding, in one place only, at the mountain. I began to worry that we'd never find our way out of the dark maze.

I paid the driver and got out, shivering in the midsummer chill, and began to walk down one street, then another. But there was nothing to be found. Only the guards, standing stock-still outside their shuttered gates; the parked cars and small trees and sleeping houses. At the end of one little road, a sharp slab of mountain, bone white and cold in the dark. I could have been back in California (or in the mock-Californian suburb where I live now in Japan).

I went on walking down the street—its straight lines, its precise edges made to insist on its distance from Bolivia—and as I did, following this path, and then that one, the rock face before me silver under the full moon, suddenly I had an eerie premonition: I'd been in this unremarkable place before. I knew its shape, the feel of it; I knew just how the streets would run, silent and straight, and then end up at the mountain.

And then, as I continued, I realized that I really had been here before: half a lifetime before—more—at the age of eighteen. I'd been traveling around South America with a schoolfriend, and at some point we had landed up in just this place. An unexceptional grid of streets that did everything they could to announce their closeness to the future.

I'd been drawn, at the time, to everything that lay outside my cozy, rectilinear neighborhood in California, and I'd come back from South America impressed by what might make an impression on any teenager: the golden, palmy beaches of Brazil; the high silence of the Altiplano, nothing but llamas and rounded hills with snow on them, a cold lake in the distance; the excited girls at the Hotel Picasso in Bogotá whom, in our innocence, we'd taken to be innocent travelers like ourselves. When I'd returned home, I'd brought back a whole carousel of slides, visible and invisible, from my adventure. And unexceptional suburban streets in La Paz had not been among them.

A quarter of a century later, though, sitting at my desk in Japan, suddenly I'd been visited, piercingly, by images of Bolivia. Its high, denim skies; the Indian women laboring up the narrow, high-walled streets past the cathedral towards the heavens; the haunted statues of Tiahuanaco, looking out on an emptiness so absolute it might have been the same a thousand years before. For some reason, I felt I had to go back there, to a place that had hardly made an impression on me, so I'd thought, when I was young.

I gathered my things and came back, at a time when all the world was suddenly talking and thinking of war, and what I found, in the dark, was an eighteen-year-old boy, with long hair down to his shoulders, in a blue-and-yellow poncho, at the end of a grueling three-month trip. It had been a weekday afternoon, I now remembered, and the two of us had followed a suggestion in *The South America Handbook* to come out to visit the new church in the suburbs. It had been a long drive from downtown—passengers had got in and got out—and by the end we were the only ones left inside the bus.

When we'd got out, we'd found that everything was closed this silent Tuesday afternoon. The church was shuttered: just the outline of the Savior striding across its roof. Around it, a new posh suburb was clearly coming up: long straight streets, and on one side, the edge of the mountains. Rob, by the end of the week, would be taking off alone, to Brasília, the Iguazú Falls; I would be in a fisherman's hut in the dark, near the mouth of the Amazon. We'd arrived, in all senses, at the end of the line.

The moment had meant next to nothing, especially in the midst of all the drama that had come before, and after, and it was almost exactly what I might never have expected to find, here on this midsummer night twenty-seven years later. And yet I could picture it all now: not so much the church as the feeling, of desolation, the air of stillness and unsettledness, the sense of a place yet to be filled in and peopled in this bright modern suburb on a silent afternoon. Straight streets in every direction, and at one edge, the mountainside.

I went back a few days later—New Year's Eve now—to see what the area looked like in broad daylight, and I found that the suburb was ablaze with karaoke parlors and restaurants. The church, in the middle of a quiet suburb, was not even mentioned in the guidebooks now. Girls in French dresses, boys in designer sunglasses were gathered outside a streetside juice stand, looking to while away a long afternoon. An Indian dwarf played a pair of panpipes at their feet, his hat extended in front of him for stray coins. The dance of rich and poor that was one of the things that had brought me here.

And yet, at the edge of the frame, another figure, more private, with long hair, looking out not at the modern grid of streets but at everything that encircled them.

The great blessing of his upbringing, Albert Camus writes in the soaring preface to his *Lyrical and Critical Essays,* was that he was born "halfway between poverty and the sun." The daily difficulty of life in his native Algeria meant that he was never very far from the lessons of infirmity and suffering that the Buddha, for one, had to leave his gilded palace to encounter; and yet the sun, the bright horizons, meant that something else was always imminent. Those two forces, hardship and possibility, became in some sense Camus's earliest playmates, which he took with him even to the curtained salons of Paris. "I feel humility," he goes on to say in the same preface, "in my heart of hearts, only in the presence of the poorest lives and the greatest adventures of the mind. Between the two is a society I find ludicrous."

What he was saying, among other things, is that he was a traveler for life, a "stranger"—to use the word forever associated with him—wherever he happened to find himself, able to bring the news from the place across the mountains to Paris, to Algiers, to everywhere. Explorations of the poorest lives became one of the great adventures of his mind. And in the process, like more and more who came after him, he threw into question what was central, what the margins, and saw how the two circle around one another like fascinated strangers, each haunted by the Other.

This is, I think, part of the impulse that moves many a traveler—the chance to confront the questions and challenges that he would never see at home. "True and serious traveling," as the great explorer and exile who never really left home, Thoreau, wrote, "is no pastime, but is as serious as the grave." These days, when we can be anywhere tomorrow (those of us in the privileged world, at least), such words can sound foolishly portentous and quaint; and yet these days, when the whole world is accessible to us, we are still finding new ways to test ourselves against Everest or Antarctica. Travel remains a journey into whatever we can't explain, or explain away.

We travel, we all know, every time we dream (or, better yet, return from a dream with a few haunted pieces we know we'll never be able to put together again); we travel when we fall, with Thomas Pynchon, into the eleven days that got lost when Wednesday, September 2, 1752, overnight as it were, became Thursday, September 14, as the Julian calendar in Britain and her colonies became the Gregorian; we travel when someone tells us the story of her life. The physical aspect of travel is, for me, the least interesting; what really draws me is the prospect of stepping out of the daylight of everything I know, into the shadows of what I don't know, and may never know. Confronted by the foreign, we grow newly attentive to the details of the world, even as we make out, sometimes, the larger outline that lies behind them. "The music of the world," as Camus, lost in Prague, observes, "finds its way more easily into this heart grown less secure. Finally stripped bare, the slightest solitary tree becomes the most tender and fragile of images."

I know in my own case that a trip has really been successful if I come back sounding strange even to myself; if, in some sense, I never come back at all, but remain up at night unsettled by what I've seen. I bring back receipts, postcards, the jottings I have made, but none of them really tells the story of what I've encountered; that remains somewhere between what I can't say and what I can't know. The smell of daphne in the little lanes of Japan in the autumn; the sound of chanting, chattering from a distant church. The red robes laid out in the sun to dry, on the whitewashed walls of a monastery, that fill me with a sudden, unanswerable sense that I've been to this place before. We travel, some of us, to slip through the curtain of the ordinary, and into the presence of whatever lies just outside our apprehension.

A temple bell sounds from across the Mekong River. A longboat drifts towards the distant shore. Children splash and laugh in the water at the foot of the steps, and, along the narrow dusty path behind us, a monk in orange robes looks down. The sun is bright, but filtered through the trees. For just a moment, for no reason I can decipher, I am in a place I know better than I should; I fall through the gratings of the conscious mind, and into a place that observes a different kind of logic.

These hauntings make up the invisible story of our lives, the shadow side of the résumé, if you like. When we sleep, as we do for perhaps a third of our days, we see not the places we know so well so much as somewhere we might have visited once, magically rearranged. Even when we're lying sleepless in our beds, trying to will ourselves into the dark, what we meet, often, are not the people who surround us every day, but a stranger, perhaps, whose eyes met ours in a café in Reykjavik twenty years ago. Something unresolved. I like the word "flights" because it can refer as much to a piano concerto as to the movements of a bird, and it reminds us that "flights of fancy" take us as far from what we know as any flights in fact.

We travel most, I mean to say, when we stumble, and we stumble most when we come to a place of poverty and need (like Haiti, perhaps, or Cambodia); and what we find in such confounding places, often, is that it is the sadness that makes the sunshine more involving or, as often, that it is the spirit and optimism of the place that make the difficulties more haunting. "The ideal travel book," Christopher Isherwood once wrote, "should be perhaps a little like a crime story, in which you're in search of something." And it's the best kind of something, I would add, if it's something you never find.

A few years ago, when America was enjoying a period of prosperity unprecedented in its history—and computers were being hailed as the unacknowledged legislators of mankind (at a time when two-thirds of the people alive had never used a telephone)—I decided to take myself off to the poorest countries in various corners of the world: to Cambodia and Laos in Asia, to Yemen in Arabia, to Haiti and Bolivia in the Americas, and to Ethiopia, Easter Island, Tibet. I didn't think that these places were more important than California; but nor was I ready to believe that they were less so. And for someone living in

California, they seemed a useful corrective to what I might otherwise assume to be real life, and a way to raise questions about what poverty really means and whether tomorrow is actually wiser than last night.

The beauty of any flight, after all, is that, as soon as we leave the ground, we leave a sense of who we are behind. The four walls that marked and enclosed our lives this morning grow smaller and still smaller, less and less distinct, till finally they disappear altogether in the grid of houses all around. We rise and rise through the clouds, into a blue stillness, and the very "we" and "I" that seemed so urgent when we awoke become as remote, as hard to take seriously, as that house far, far below, now invisible.

The particular blessing of the modern moment, for me, is that such flights are more and more accessible, even to those who never travel. The Other is everywhere today, not least on our front doorsteps. We step outside our houses and are surrounded by the colors and rites of the place across the mountains. Ghosts and talismans and ancient superstitions are all around us; look outside your window, and you may see a dead chicken placed ceremonially at the center of a crossroads. A foreign mumbling is coming through the walls, from the new neighbor, and the signs on the store down the street dance and swirl as in a suq in North Africa. The modern, shifting world has brought disorientation home to us, and mystery and strangeness; even in the most familiar places we may come upon something unsettling, just through the alien presence at our side (I go into a church in Florence, everyday as the morning to me, and the friend I've brought with me from Japan suddenly stiffens, and runs out, her heart assaulted by the strangeness of a place I would never think twice about).

This flooding of the foreign into our living rooms—our bedrooms—is not always conducive to a sense of calm; all the spirits we like to keep locked up—suspicion, defensiveness, fear—suddenly rear their heads. A stranger is always at our door, nowadays, with an offer, an inquiry, and we don't know what to make of him. The Other brings alien rhythms, smells, and spices to the neighborhood, and we're in the dark even when the room is brightly lit.

And so I decided to put together a sequence of explorations that told of journeys that left me shaking in some way, whether they came through books I happened to pick up, or through trips to southern Oman. My aim, when recording them, was to try to carry the reader off, as I had been carried off, into a sense of strangeness, and into the expanded sense of possibility that strangeness sometimes brings. The chapters circle back, again and again, to certain places and the questions they inspire—the questions I take everywhere with me, of possession, of New Year's Day, of the play of light and dark—but their end point, always, is the deeper question of what we take to be real and how, as Camus puts it, we put the sunlight in the same frame as the suffering. I take the long drive to Dharamsala, the small Tibetan settlement in the foothills of the Himalaya, and the Dalai Lama tells me that exile, suffering, loss—everything—is, if seen in the right light, a blessing and a teaching. I go that same year to Cambodia and find myself encircled by a darkness I can't write off.

I walk out sometimes on October mornings in Japan, the sky as cloudless as in the High Himalaya, the first touch of winter bringing an edge of chill, a sense of dark, to the afternoons, and all I can think of, on occasion, is the end of Shakespeare's early comedy *Love's Labour's Lost*. Berowne has charmed himself and us with his flights of fancy, and he is minutes away from escorting his paramour offstage, as comedy decrees, when suddenly a messenger appears, in black, out of nowhere. The princess's father—he begins. Is dead, she says, knowing what he will say before he says it. Moments before its culmination, the comedy is upended, and everything is left wide open.

If he would truly have her hand, his love now says, turning to Berowne—though they had been about to walk off together, into a happy ending—he must take himself away from her for a year. To let Time try him, in part—to outstay the impatience of his youth—but also to see how his love of words can help the "groaning wretches" and "speechless sick" of an infirmary.

"To move wild laughter in the throat of death?" he says. That's hardly possible. In that case, she responds, what use are any of his words? Either he must forswear his language, or find a tonic use for it.

I walk through the chill, sharp streets, the sky quite cloudless, the leaves turning, and what I see is what the play is saying, in a different key: everything falls away from us—the light, the dark, the warm afternoons—and all we can do is cry out in affirmation of our joy.

SUN
AFTER
DARK

I will visit a place entirely
other than myself.
Whether it is the future
or the past need not be
decided in advance.

—SUSAN SONTAG

A

GATHERING

AROUND

A

PERPLEXITY

In the falling mountain darkness, I pull my car off the high winding road, into a rough parking lot, and a man comes out to greet me: an older man, stooped a little and shaven-headed, in tattered black gown and woolen cap and glasses. He extends a hand, gives me a bow and, picking up my case, leads me off to a cabin. He worries about my "long drive," asks if I'll be okay here, heats up a pot of tea and slices some fresh bread for me. As night falls, he tells me to feel at home and says he knows a young woman he thinks I should be married to.

Then, since I will need some special clothes to join him in the austerities for which he has invited me, he leads me, this Old Testament gentleman, off into the chill, unlit night, to collect a gown and cap and pair of canvas sneakers for me. His home is a markedly simple place, a small black welcome mat outside its door. Inside are a narrow single bed, a tiny mirror, a dirty old carpet, and some puppies cavorting under the legend "Friends Are All Welcome."

Farther inside, a pair of scissors, a few Kleenexes, a small shoulder bag with a Virgin Airlines tag attached to it, and, on a chest of drawers, a menorah. "This place is really quite a trip," he tells me, smiling. "You enter a kind of science-fiction universe, which has no beginning and no end." His own ragged gown, I notice, is held together with safety pins. The small Technics synthesizer in the next room is unplugged.

Leading me out into the dark, he climbs a steep path to where there are tall pine trees, and the outline of monks in the distance, a thousand stars. We slip into a cold, empty room, and he gives me instructions on how to sit. "The bottom half—the legs—should be really strong," he says. "The rest should be fluid."

Then, assessing my posture as serviceable, he leads me out into the mountain dark and into the *zendo,* or meditation hall, next door. Thirty or so figures, all in black, are sitting stock-still in the night. They are in the throes of a winter retreat, *rohatsu,* in which they will sit like this, all but uninterruptedly, for seven days. Monks patrol the aisles with sticks, ready to hit anyone who threatens to drop off. Every forty-five minutes or so, the practitioners are allowed to break from their *zazen* positions to relieve themselves in buckets in the woods, or in rough outhouses known and feared throughout the Zen community. Most of them use the breaks, however, to continue their meditation unbroken, marching, in spellbound, silent Indian file, round and around a central pine tree. My host, I notice, is probably thirty years older than most of the fresh-faced young men and women in attendance; yet as they walk around the tree, at top speed, he seems at least thirty years stronger, too.

At 2:00 a.m., after I head back to my cabin to get some sleep, there's a knock on my door, and a flashlight in the dark, and it's the rabbinical-seeming elderly man again, ready to vault up rough stone paths to join in morning chants. For half an hour or so, to the beat of a steadily pounded drum, the assembled students race through twenty-four pages of Japanese syllabary that mean nothing to them—my host, like many others, reciting the entire *Heart Sutra* from memory. Then he leads me back through the frosty night to his cabin, to show me the ninth-century text on which we'll be hearing a *teisho,* or Zen discourse. It's a fearless scripture, as bracing as a sudden blow to the skull. "Anything you may find through seeking," the Zen master Rinzai warns, "will be only a wild fox spirit."

The light has come back to the austere settlement, and the huge boulders outside my room look as if they're buried in snow when I hear a knock again, and follow my sleepless host up again, through the black-and-white silence, to hear the *roshi,* or teacher of this community, deliver his daily talk. A small round figure in huge orange robes comes in, and two attendants help him onto a kind of throne. "What is this thing called love?" the man says, speaking in the old-fashioned tones of his northern Japanese dialect, translated by a young apprentice. "A child can befriend a dog and lick its rear end. Is that love? Is love just shaking hands? Dogs and cats and insects mate; is that love?

"You've been hypnotized," he goes on. "You've got to take your mind to the laundry. Get it clean." And, he concludes, "When a man is with a woman, he has to occupy her fully."

Afterwards, we head out into what is now a dazzling blue-sky day. "Nine o'clock," says Leonard Cohen, a penetrating glint in his eye, "and we've had several lives already today."

· · ·

Leonard Cohen is for most of us a figure of the dark, sitting alone sometime after midnight and exploring the harsh truths of suffering and loneliness. It's four in the morning, the end of December, as one of his mournful songs begins, though in his recent work, like Thomas Merton in his way, he has seemed to look so intensely at the dark that something else comes through (there is a crack, a crack in everything, he sings, and that's how the light gets in). His songs and poems have always been about letting go and giving things up, the voluntary poverty of a refugee from comfort.

Yet even those who see in him an explorer of chosen limits and the dark—even those who know that he turned down the Governor General's Award for Poetry in Canada when he was thirty-four, lived in a bare house on the Greek island of Hydra that he bought with a $1,500 inheritance, and wrote, scored, and directed an entire film called *I Am a Hotel*—may be surprised to hear that the definitive ladies' man and husky poet of the morning after is living now, year-round, in the Mount Baldy Zen Center, 6,250 feet above sea level, in the dark San Gabriel Mountains behind Los Angeles, serving, as he says, as "cook, chauffeur, and sometimes drinking-buddy" to a ninety-one-year-old Japanese man with whom he shares few words.

Cohen has, in fact, been a friend of Joshu Sasaki ever since 1973, though he has not made a fuss about it, and votaries will get clues to this part of his existence only from a couple of tiny elliptical vignettes in his 1978 book, *Death of a Lady's Man*, and occasional songs—for example, "If It Be Your Will"—that, like his 1984 collection of psalms, *Book of Mercy*, express absolute submission. Apart from a twenty-six-year-old son, Adam, and a twenty-three-year-old daughter, Lorca, the Japanese *roshi* seems to be the one still point in Cohen's endlessly turning life, and now the singer accompanies the man he calls his friend to Zen centers from Vienna to Puerto Rico, and goes through punishing retreats each month in which he does nothing but sit *zazen,* twenty-four hours a day for seven days on end.

The rest of the time, he works around the Zen center, shoveling snow, scrubbing floors, and—most enthusiastically— working around the kitchen (he tells me, with mischievous pride, that he has a certificate from the County of San Bernardino that qualifies him to work as waiter, busboy, or cook). For the monk here known as Jikan (or "Silent One"), all the things he's famous for—a command of words, beautiful suits, a hunger for ideas, and a hypnotist's ease at charming the world—are thrown aside. "In the *zendo,*" he tells me, not unhappily, "all of this disappears." ("This" referring, I think, to his name, his past, the life he carries around within him.) "You don't notice if this woman's beautiful or ugly. If that man smells or doesn't smell. Whoever you're sitting next to, you just see their pain. And when you're sitting, you feel nothing but the pain. And sometimes it goes, and then it's back again. And you can't think of anything else. Just the pain." He pauses (and the *chanteur/enchanteur* slips out again). "And, of course, it's the same with other kinds of pain, like broken hearts."

The icon who's been entertained and idolized by everyone from Prince Charles and Georges Pompidou to Joni Mitchell and Michelle Phillips; the regular visitor to the top of the European charts who's inspired not one tribute album (like most legends) but a dozen; the Officer of the Order of Canada recently described, in *The United States of Poetry,* as "perhaps the continent's most successful poet" seems to thrive on this. He's too happy to write anymore, he tells me soon after I arrive (though, one day later, he's showing me things he's writing, towards a new *Book of Longing*). And though the face is still strikingly reminiscent of Dustin Hoffman—especially if he were acting as Harold Bloom—it's well hidden in the bobble cap that his *roshi* "commanded" him to wear. "This whole practice is mostly about terrifying you," he says cheerfully. "But there's a lot to be gained in those terrors. It gets you so efficiently into a certain place."

And the place is one that Cohen has been journeying towards all his life, in a sense. "There's a bias against religious virtue here," he assures me, grinning, one morning, as bells toll outside and I smell sweet incense in the air and hear clappers knocking in the distance, "and it's very appealing. So you never have the feeling that it's Sunday school. And you never have the feeling that you're abandoning some cavalier life, or getting into some goody-goody enterprise. Not at all. Not at all." When a Buddhist magazine recently asked Cohen to conduct an interview with Sasaki, he gladly agreed, provided they could talk about "wine, women, and money." And, to be sure, we've hardly been introduced for the first time before the disarming sinner-songwriter is using "pussy" and *"shunyata"* in the same sentence.

It's not so much that Cohen has given up the world—he still has a duplex that he bought with two friends near the Jewish district on Fairfax (where his daughter currently lives), and when I visit him at two one morning, I hear the crackle of a transistor radio in his bedroom. The man with a gift for being in tune with the times is still doing things like providing the songs that are heard on the sound track of Oliver Stone's state-of-the-art *Natural Born Killers,* appearing at Rebecca De Mornay's side at the Academy Awards, and inspiring a new generation of grunge poets—to the point where Kurt Cobain famously sang, "Give me a Leonard Cohen afterworld so I can sigh eternally." But he's nonetheless managed to come to L.A., archetypal center of spoiled sunshine, and turn it into a high, cold mountain training more rigorous than the army.

In some ways, he's been there since the beginning. His songs, after all, have always been about obedience and war, pain and attention and surrender, and he's always seemed a curiously old-fashioned, even forbidding figure who abhors clutter and goes it alone and yearns to be on his knees as well as on his toes—focused and penetrating and wild. The dark skies and spare spaces and mythic shapes around Mount Baldy feel uncannily like the landscape of a Leonard Cohen song.

Besides, the self-styled "Voice of Suffering" has never chosen to diversify his themes; he just goes deeper and deeper into them. The refrain that lights up his recent song "Democracy" actually appears in his novel *Beautiful Losers,* from thirty-two years ago; the poem he recently recited as a prologue to the album *Rare on Air,* volume 1, was one he wrote for his first book, composed in part when he was in high school. Even thirty years ago, when he was known as a woman-hungry, acid-dropping, enfant terrible provocateur, he was writing, "Prayer is translation. A man translates himself into a child asking for all there is in a language he has barely mastered."

And for half a century almost, he's been slipping in and out of view, playing games with the entity known as "Leonard Cohen." There's the small, upper-middle-class Jewish kid taking lessons in hypnotism, forming a country-and-western band called "The Buckskin Boys" and, while studying English at McGill, reciting verse over jazz at midnight like some wintry Kerouac. There's the slightly older figure, scrupulously dissolute, and already the author of six books when he read his poem "Suzanne" over the phone to Judy Collins and she persuaded him to sing it himself, which led to his appearing, this uncertain-seeming theologian, at the Monterey Jazz Festival, at the Isle of Wight Festival, and on the client list of John Hammond (the man who discovered both Dylan and Springsteen). There's the leading young poet in Canada who not only delivered lectures on "Loneliness and History" and composed a whole opera in the sixteenth-century verse form of *The Faerie Queene*, but also lost his rights to "Suzanne," with the result that his first and most famous song to this day brings him no money at all.

He lived on the Greek island with his Norwegian love in the 1960s. He acquired a "small, cupboard-sized room" in the Chelsea Hotel, where Joan Baez, Bob Dylan, and Jimi Hendrix came through now and then. He took over a twelve-hundred-acre homestead in Franklin, Tennessee (rented from the writer of "Bye, Bye Love" for seventy-five dollars a month), and posed for photos in a Stetson. He got dissected by the novelist Michael Ondaatje in a book-length work of literary criticism; sold excerpts from his work to *Cavalier,* the skin magazine; appeared at one concert riding a white horse; and greeted an audience in Hamburg with the cry *"Sieg Heil!"*

Cohen showed, in fact, an almost disquieting readiness to live out every romantic myth, from staying in a garret to moving to Greece (for its "philosophic climate"), to telling all his women that being true to them meant being untrue to his Muse. What this provoked, understandably, was a sense in many quarters that he was brashly courting success by pretending to ignore it. "If you listen carefully," the *New York Times* said in 1973, "you are sometimes rewarded with a poet's profound thoughts, sometimes with a pop star's put-on." Undeterred, Cohen continued to subvert his success with puckish gestures, following a book of poems called *The Spice-Box of Earth* with another called *Flowers for Hitler,* scribbling up aphorisms on walls—"Change is the only aphrodisiac"—and then ascribing them to the Kama Sutra. Even his career seemed a game he was playing, as he teamed up with, of all people, Phil Spector, for the 1977 album *Death of a Ladies' Man,* in which dark and serious inquiries into the nature of the soul got buried under a foot-thumping "Wall of Sound." (Cohen himself called the album "a grotesque masterpiece.") The final irony was that this overblown Vegas casino of a production may in fact have paved the way for the fuller, richer sounds of later albums that brought Cohen surging back onto the charts in his mid-fifties.

Indeed, Cohen always seemed to have a gift for the last word. By the 1990s, the magazines that had long found him an irre-sistible target for put-downs were publishing articles with titles like "7 Reasons Leonard Cohen Is the Next Best Thing to God." The head of one of New York's most prestigious publishing houses was telling me that Cohen had "the best design sense of anyone I've met," and the man who hadn't performed live in New York for ten years was number one in Norway for seventeen weeks. Even the *New York Times,* his unwearying opponent for twenty-five years, was concluding, in 1995, "He is pretty extraor-dinary, when all is said and done."

Now, as we sit in his cabin one cold December morning, a string of Christmas lights twinkling sadly from the roadside shack across the street, "Mike ♥ Suzie" scrawled into the concrete, he's telling me that he makes no claims to piety or knowledge: his training here is just a useful response to the "predicament" of his life. This "connection—the unavoidable presence of the Other—has driven us to religion," he says, explaining why he thinks "the great religion is the great work of art." We "form ourselves around these problems," he goes on. "These problems exist prior to us, and we gather ourselves, almost molecularly, we gather ourselves around these perplexities. And that's what a human is: a gathering around a perplexity."

He sips some coffee from a cup with the logo of *The Future* on it, beside him the thick notebooks in which poems hundreds of verses long will get condensed, often, into a single six-verse song. Around us, as we sit, almost nothing else except a bottle of Sparkletts water, a few candles, a toothbrush, and, tucked into a light switch, a picture of the Winged Victory. Cohen has not slept, most likely, for six days. "It's driven us to art," he says, returning to his theme of the Other. "I mean, it's so perplexing, the humiliations, the glories that are so abundant, and it's such a dangerous undertaking. I was just looking through my notebooks, and I saw something nice. It was 'I set out for love, but I did not know I'd be caught in the grip of an undertow. To be swept to a shore, where the sea needs to go, with a child in my arms, and a chill in my soul, and my heart the size of a begging-bowl.'"

And even on this lofty perch, with nothing visible but rock and tree and occasional sign prohibiting the throwing of snowballs, he doesn't deny the "fixed self" that awaits him whenever he comes down from the mountain, and, in fact, goes out of his way to deride his presence on the mountaintop. "Everyone here is fucked-up and desperate," he says brightly. "That's why they're here. You don't come to a place like this unless you're desperate." Yet over and over, amidst the calculated irreverence, the gamesmanship and the crazy-wisdom subversiveness—one of the reasons he became a monk two years ago, he says, was "Roshi wanted me to do so for tax purposes"—I see something touching and genuine coming through. Leonard Cohen, I realize, is really trying, with all his body and his soul, to simplify himself as strictly as he does his word-strong verses.

One morning, at dawn, as we talk about Van Morrison and Norman Mailer and how "living in England is like living in a cabbage," Cohen gets to talking of Cuba, and the time, just after the Revolution, when he was walking along the beach in his Canadian Army khaki shorts with his camping knife, imagining himself the only North American on the island, and got arrested as the first member of an invading force.

"So anyway, there I was, on the beach in Varadero, speculating on my destiny, when suddenly I found myself surrounded by sixteen soldiers with guns. They arrested me and the only words I knew at the time were *'Amistad de pueblo.'* So I kept saying *'Amigo! Amistad de pueblo!'* and finally they started greeting me. And they gave me a necklace of shells and a necklace of bullets and everything was great—"

Then, suddenly, he stops. "What time is it?"

I tell him and he says, "I shouldn't be talking about my adventures when we're about to listen to a wonderful *teisho.*" And Leonard Cohen disappears into the black-robed disciple again, and into a reverent silence.

Another day, another tale as short and abstract and mythic, almost, as any of his ballads about worshiping at the altar of beauty, as he suddenly volunteers to tell me about his last girl-friend. "When I met Rebecca [De Mornay]," he says, "all kinds of thoughts came into my mind, as how could they not when faced with a woman of such beauty? And they got crisscrossed in my mind. But she didn't let it go further than that: my mind. And it did. And finally she saw I was a guy who just couldn't come across."

" 'Come across'?"

"In the sense of being a husband and having more children and the rest." He stops. "And she was right, of course. But she was kind enough to forgive me. I had breakfast with her the other day, and I told her, 'I know why you forgave me. Because I really, really tried.' And she said, 'Yes.' "

End of story, end of song.

At times, as I listened, spellbound against my will by this man with beautiful manners and a poet's rare diction, moving back and forth between hippie existentialist and Old World scholar, now referring to "bread" and "tokes" and "beating the rap," now talking in a high-pitched tone of "ancient" and "dismal" and "predicament," I could see the coyote trickster who's been working the press for three decades or more. I felt disconcerted, almost, by his very niceness, his openness, his courtesy, as he continually kept thanking me for "being kind enough to come here," and tended to my every need as if I were the celebrity and he the poor journalist, referring to "what you're nice enough to call my career." I felt there was something excessive to his modesty, his unusually articulate and quick-witted sentences bemoaning his lack of articulacy and sharpness ("I'm sorry. You get this kind of spaciness at moments in retreats. They say *zazen* brings short-term memory loss"), his claiming not to know, after twenty years in L.A., how long it takes to drive to Santa Barbara.

I saw the seasoned seducer whom his friend Anjelica Huston recently called "part wolf, part angel," and sensed that he could put "confidence" and "artist" together as easily as "pilgrim" and "mage." Certainly a man so meticulous in clothes and manner was not going to be careless in his presentation of self—was, in fact, likely to be a master-craftsman of self.

Yet the trouble was, Cohen seemed more wise to this than anyone. "Secretly," he told me cheerily, "the sin of pride as it's manifested here is that we feel we're like the Marines of the spiritual world: tougher, more reckless, more daring, more brave." Asked about his early years, he confesses, "I think I was more interested in the poetic life and everything around it than the thing itself." Nominating himself as "one of the great whiners," he says that the *roshi* looks at him sometimes and says, "Attention to the world: need more Buddhism!"

And so, as time passes, I really do begin to feel I am watching a complex man trying to come clear, a still jangled, sometimes angry soul making a heroic attempt to reduce itself to calm. As day passes into night and day again, he comes into focus, and out again, like the sun behind clouds, now blazing with a lucent, high intensity, now more like the difficult brooder you might imagine from the records. "He's a tiger," I remember a woman in New York telling me, "a very complicated man. Complicated in a very grown-up way. I mean, he makes Dylan seem childish." The first time she met him, she explained, he congratulated her on a book she'd written. As their meal went on, he added, "Your writing is a lot more interesting than you are."

Cruelty has always been as disconcerting a part of his package as perversity. Yet when I talked to the people who tour with him I felt I was speaking to the Apostles. "I don't think I've ever met anyone as gracious, as graceful, as generous as Leonard," said Perla Batalla, who has been singing with him for eight years. "Once I'd been out on the road with Leonard, I couldn't go out with anyone else." His other backup singer, Julie Christensen, left a newborn baby at home to go out on tour with him—having seen her friends who'd been in his band come back "changed, philosophically changed, really on this kind of heightened awareness level." His longtime accompanist, Jennifer Warnes, even recorded a whole album of Cohen songs she wanted to rebring before the public.

All of them talk of how Cohen the singer seems of a piece with Cohen the Zen practitioner, making them sing and sing and sing the same song till sometimes they'll break into tears, and wearing them out with his indefatigable three-hour, twelve-encore concerts. But all speak of his tours as if they were a kind of spiritual training. "He'll give the same attention to the president of the country or to someone who's just walked up to him on the street," says Batalla, recalling how he rode on the bus like just another technician. Others mention his racing off to buy aspirin for them when they're sick, or inviting them to his hotel room at night to drink hot chocolate made with water from the sink.

"In the ancient concert halls of Europe," says Christensen, "you got this feeling that you'd really have to run if you weren't telling the truth. It was a mystery bigger than me, and if I'd figured it out, I would be bigger than it." Then, almost sheepishly, she adds, "I thought that kind of thing was corny before I toured with Leonard." Batalla sometimes visits his home just to sit in absolute silence with her boss.

And so the days on the mountain go on, and every day at dawn young monks with clean, pure faces appear at my door with trays of food, and every day, when I visit Cohen in his cabin, he gives me green tea in a wineglass, or shows me paintings—flowing nudes and haggard self-portraits—he's done on his computer, or reads me poems about the dissolution of self from a book he is putting together, which, like all his best work, sound like love songs or prayers or both, addressed to a goddess or to God.

One morning, in his bathroom, I come upon *The Shambhala Dictionary of Buddhism and Zen.*

"I like the fact they distinguish between Buddhism and Zen," he says when I come out.

"What is the difference?"

He disappears—good Zen solution—into the bathroom to clean cups.

Another day, as the retreat is drawing to a close, the sky above my window grey and shriven and severe, he shows up with his hands dirty from fixing his toilet, and I try to get him to talk about his writing. "For me," he says, his voice soft and beautiful, with a trace of Canada still hiding inside it, "the process is really more like a bear stumbling into a beehive or a honey cache: I'm stumbling right into it and getting stuck, and it's delicious and it's horrible and I'm in it. And it's not very graceful and it's very awkward and it's very painful"—you can hear the cadences of his songs here—"and yet there's something inevitable about it." But most of the writers he admires, preempting one's criticism again, "are just incredible messes, as human beings. Wonderful and invigorating company, but I pity their wives and their husbands and their children."

A crooked smile.

As for the songs, "I've always held the song in high regard," he says, "because songs have got me through so many sinks of dishes and so many humiliating courting events." Sometimes, he goes on, holding me with his commanding eloquence, his ill-shaven baritone compounded of Gauloises, Courvoisier, and a lifetime of late nights, he'll catch a snatch of one of his songs on the radio, "and I'll think: these songs are really good. And it's really wonderful that they have been written, and more wonderful that they should have found a place in the heart. And sometimes I'll hear my voice, and I'll think: this guy has got to be the great comedian of his generation. These are hilarious: hilariously inept, hilariously solemn and out of keeping with the times; hilariously inappropriate."

A line he's used for years, I know, but still more than you'd expect from a man whose songs are covered by Willie Nelson and Billy Joel. "To me," he continues, scraping at his sneakers with a knife, "the kind of thing I like is that you write a song, and it slips into the world, and they forget who wrote it. And it moves and it changes, and you hear it again three hundred years later, some women washing their clothes in a stream, and one of them is humming this tune." His conversation like the outline of a ballad.

At last, as the 168 hours come to an end, I walk up the mountain to join the students in what will be their final session of *zazen,* the stars above the pines thicker than I have seen in thirty years of living in Southern California. By now, nearly all of them are exhausted to the point of breakdown—or breakthrough—some of them with open wounds on their feet, others nodding off at every turn, still others lit up and charged as electrical wires.

And then, at two in the morning, on the longest night of the year, suddenly the silence breaks, and people talk, and laugh, and return to being maths professors and doctors and writers again as they collect the letters that have been accumulating for them, and drink tea, and, in the great exhalation, I can hear a woman saying, in exultation, in relief, "Better than drugs!"

In his sepulchral cabin, Cohen breaks out the cognac and serves an old friend and me gefilte fish, Hebrew National salami, and egg-and-onion matzohs from a box. The two of them look like battle-hardened veterans—"non-commissioned officers," as the friend says—and it's not hard to see how this celebrated lady-killer called an early backup band "The Army" and one of his sweetest records "an anti-pacifist recording."

Yet even at his most ragged here, he seems a long way away from the one who cried out, so pitifully, on his 1973 live album, "I can't stand who I am." Leonard Cohen has always seemed, or tried, to inhabit a higher zone of sorts, and one that his parable-like songs, his alchemical symbols, and his constant harking back to Abraham and David and Isaac only compound. In trying to marry Babylon with Bethlehem, in reading women's bodies with the obsessiveness of a Talmudic scholar, in giving North America a raffish tilt so that he's always been closer to Jacques Brel or Georges Moustaki than to Bob Dylan, he's been trying, over and over, to find ceremony without sanctimony and discipline without dogma. Where else should he be, where else could he be, than in a military-style ritualized training that allows him to put Old Testament words to a country-and-western beat and write songs that sound like first-person laments written by God?

"I feel," says Cohen a little later, when we're alone, "we're in a very shabby moment, and neither the literary nor the musical experience really has its finger on the pulse of our crisis. From my point of view, we're in the midst of a Flood: a Flood of biblical proportions. It's both exterior and interior—at this point it's more devastating on the interior level—but it's leaking into the real world. And this Flood is of such enormous and biblical proportions that I see everybody holding on in their individual way to an orange crate, to a piece of wood, and we're passing each other in this swollen river that has pretty well taken down all the landmarks, and pretty well overturned everything we've got. And people insist, under the circumstances, on describing themselves as 'liberal' or 'conservative.' It seems to me completely mad."

Of course, he says, impatiently, he can't explain what he's doing here. "I don't think anybody really knows why they're doing anything. If you stop someone on the subway and say, 'Where are you going—in the deepest sense of the word?' you can't really expect an answer. I really don't know why I'm here. It's a matter of 'What else would I be doing?' Do I want to be Frank Sinatra, who's really great, and do I want to have great retrospectives of my work? I'm not really interested in being the oldest folksinger around.

"Would I be starting a new marriage with a young woman and raising another family? Well, I hated it when it was going on"—signs of the snarl beneath the chuckle—"so maybe I would feel better about it now. But I don't think so.

"What would I be doing? Finding new drugs, buying more expensive wine? I don't know. This seems to me the most luxurious and sumptuous response to the emptiness of my own existence.

"I think that's the real deep entertainment," he concludes. "Religion. Real profound and voluptuous and delicious entertainment. The real feast that is available to us is within this activity. Nothing touches it." He smiles his godfatherly smile. "Except if you're courtin'. If you're young, the hormonal thrust has its own excitement."

Before I leave, he catches my eye, and his voice turns soft.

"We are gathered here," he says, "around a very, very old man, who may outlive all of us, and who may go tomorrow. So that gives an urgency to the practice. Everybody, including Roshi, is practicing with a kind of passionate diligence. It touches my heart. It makes me proud to be part of this community."

Before I leave the following morning, the *roshi* invites me, with Cohen, to his cabin for lunch. It's a typically eclectic meal, of noodles and curry, taken quietly and simply, in a small sunlit dining area. As ever when the *roshi* is around, Cohen sits absolutely humble and silent in one corner, all the tension emptied out of his face; everything about him is light, like a clear glass once the liquid's drained.

He tells me a little about how he was once fascinated by Persian miniatures. He talks of the intensity of "living in a world of samples." He cleans up around the kitchen, and asks his old friend, very gently, if he's tired. When we go out into the parking lot, a woman comes up and starts telling him how much his songs have meant to her, and Cohen gives her his warmest smile and leaves her with a kind of blessing. "A practice like this," he tells me, "and I think everyone here would say the same thing, you could only do for love."

"So if it weren't for the *roshi*, you wouldn't be here?" I ask.

"If it weren't for the *roshi*, I wouldn't be."

And as I set off down the mountain—listening with new ears now to the old songs, and seeing the shadow of an old Japanese man behind the love songs and the ballads about "the few who forgive what you do and the fewer who don't even care"—I realize that the whole stay has affected me more powerfully than any trip I've taken in years. Why? Mostly, I think, because of a sense of the deep bond between Sasaki and Cohen, and the way neither seems to need anything from the other, yet each allows the other to be deeper than he might be otherwise. "Roshi knows me for who I am," Cohen had said, "and he doesn't want me to be any other. 'International Man,' 'Culture Man,' he calls me; he knows I am an 'International Man.'" And, by all accounts, he will take everything Cohen brings him—his selfishness, his anger, his ambition, his sins—and, while holding him to them, accept him.

It's touching in a way: the man who has been the poet laureate of those in flight, who has never found in his sixty-three years a woman he can marry or a home he won't desert, the connoisseur of betrayal and self-tormenting soul who claimed, twenty-five years ago, that he had "torn everyone who reached out for me," and who ended his most recent collection of writings with a prayer for "the precious ones I overthrew for an education in the world"—the man, in fact, who became an international heartthrob while singing "So Long" and "Goodbye"—has finally found something he hasn't abandoned and a love that won't let him down.

"Roshi said something to me the other day that I like," Cohen told me just before I left. "'The older you get, the lonelier you become; and the deeper the love that you need.'" For the old and the deep and the lonely, change, it seems, may not be the only aphrodisiac.

1998

MAKING

KINDNESS

STAND

TO

REASON

Though the Dalai Lama is increasingly famous as a speaker, his real gift, you see as soon as you begin talking to him, is for listening. And though he is most celebrated around the world these days for his ability to talk to halls large enough to stage a Bon Jovi concert, his special strength is to address twenty thousand people—Buddhists and grandmothers and kids alike—as if he were talking to each one alone, in the language she can best understand. The Dalai Lama's maxims are collected and packaged now as books to carry in your handbag, as calendar items and as advertising slogans, but the heart of the man exists, I think, in silence. In his deepest self he is that being who sits alone each day at dawn, eyes closed, reciting prayers, with all his heart, for his Chinese oppressors, his Tibetan people, and all sentient beings.

Yet the curiosity of the Fourteenth Dalai Lama's life—one of the things that have made it seem at once a parable and a kind of koan—is that he has had to pursue his spiritual destiny, for more than half a century, almost entirely in the world (and, in fact, in a political world whose god is Machiavelli). His story is an all but timeless riddle about the relation of means to ends: in order to protect six million people, and to preserve a rare and long-protected culture that is only years away from extinction, he has had to pose for endless photos with models and let his speeches be broadcast on the floors of London dance clubs. To some extent, he has had to enter right into the confusion and chaos of the Celebrity Age in order to fulfill his monastic duties. The question that he carries with him everywhere he goes is the simple one of whether the world will scar him before he elevates it: in three centuries, after all, no Ocean of Wisdom, Holder of the White Lotus, and protector of the Land of Snows before him has ever served as guest editor of French *Vogue*.

I went to visit the Dalai Lama in Dharamsala not long ago, as I have done at regular intervals since my teens. I took the rickety Indian Airlines flight from Delhi to Amritsar, itself a restricted war zone (because it houses the Sikh stronghold of the Golden Temple), and from there took a five-hour taxi ride up into the foothills of the Himalaya. As I approached the distant settlement on a ridge above a little town—the roads so jam-packed with scooters and bicycles and cows that often we could hardly move (the Dalai Lama has, for security reasons, to drive for ten hours along such roads every time he wishes to take a flight)—Dharamsala came into view, and then disappeared, like a promise of liberation, or some place that didn't really exist. Most of the time—the car collapsing on a mountain road, a group of villagers assembling to push it hopefully forwards, night falling, and each turn seeming to take us farther from the string of lights far off—I felt sure we'd never get there.

As soon as you arrive at the dusty, bedraggled place, however, you realize you are very far from fairy tale, in the realm of suffering and old age and death. Windows are broken and paths half paved in the rainy little village where the Dalai Lama has made his home for more than half his life now; even the happy cries and songs of the orphans at the Tibetan Children's Village on one side of town have a slightly wistful air, as the sun sets behind the nearby mountains. When you call the Dalai Lama's office, you will hear that "All circuits are busy" or that the five-digit number changed yesterday. Sometimes my calls got cut off in mid-sentence, amidst a blur of static; sometimes I got put on hold—for all eternity, it seemed—to the tune of "London Bridge Is Falling Down."

It is, therefore, perhaps the perfect paradoxical setting for a humble monk who lives alone when he is not being sought out by Goldie Hawn or Harrison Ford. In the antechamber to his living room, after you've been checked by a Tibetan guard and then an Indian one, you sit under a certificate of Honorary Citizenship from Orange County, an award from the Rotary Club of Dharamsala, and a plaque commemorating an honorary professorship from Kalmyk State University. Ceremonial masks, Hindu deities, and pietàs shine down on you. On one wall is a huge, blown-up photo of the Tibetan capital of Lhasa, showing that the palace where the Dalai Lama once lived is now ringed by discos, brothels, and a new Chinese prison, with high-rises dwarfing the old Tibetan houses.

The Dalai Lama has a singular gift for seeing the good in everything and seeming unfazed by all the madness that swirls around him; he is always thoroughly human and always thoroughly himself. Sometimes, as you wait to see him, his exuberant new friend, a very puppyish German shepherd, runs into the room and starts jumping over a group of startled Tibetan monks here for a serious discussion, licking the faces of the Buddhist teachers before romping off into the garden again. Sometimes a pair of English hippies is in attendance, since the Dalai Lama is ready to take advice and instruction from anyone (and knows—such is the poignancy of his life—that even the most disorganized traveler may know, firsthand, more about contemporary Tibet, and the state of his people, than he does). When a photographer asks him to take off his glasses, pose with this expression, sit this way or sit that, he seizes the chance to ask the young man about what he saw when he photographed uprisings in Lhasa many years before.

As I sit across from him in his room with its large windows, looking out on pine-covered slopes and the valley below—*thangkas* all around us on the walls—the Dalai Lama makes himself comfortable, cross-legged in his armchair, and serves me tea. He always notices when my cup is empty before I do. He rocks back and forth as he speaks, the habit acquired, one realizes, over decades of punishing hours-long meditation sessions, often in the cold. And part of his disarming power (the result, no doubt, of all that meditation and the dialectics of which he is a master) is that he launches stronger criticisms against himself than even his fiercest enemies might.

When first he met Shoko Asahara, he tells me one day (referring to the man who later planned the planting of deadly sarin gas in the Tokyo subway system), he was genuinely moved by the man's seeming devotion to the Buddha: tears would come into the Japanese teacher's eyes when he spoke of Buddha. But to endorse Asahara, as he did, was, the Dalai Lama quickly says, "a mistake. Due to ignorance! So, this proves"—and he breaks into his full-throated laugh—"I'm not a 'Living Buddha'!" Another day, talking about the problems of present-day Tibet, he refers to the fact that there are "too many prostrations there," and then, erupting into gales of infectious laughter again, he realizes that he should have said "too much prostitution" (though, in fact, as he knows, "too many prostrations" may actually constitute a deeper problem). He'd love to delegate some responsibility to his deputies, he says frankly, "but, even if some of my cabinet ministers wanted to give public talks, nobody would come."

The result is that it all comes down to him. The Dalai Lama is rightly famous for his unstoppable warmth, his optimism, and his forbearance—"the happiest man in the world," as one journalist-friend calls him—and yet his life has seen more difficulty and sadness than that of anyone I know. He's representing the interests of six million largely unworldly and disenfranchised people against a nation of 1.2 billion whom nearly all the world is trying to court. He's the guest of a huge nation with problems of its own, which would be very grateful if he just kept quiet. He travels the world constantly (on a yellow refugee's "identity certificate"), and, though regarded by most as a leader equivalent to Mother Teresa or the Pope, is formally as ostracized as Muammar Qaddafi or Kim Jong Il. He is excited when meeting Britain's Queen Mother—because he remembers, from his boyhood days, seeing news clips of her tending to the poor of London during the Blitz—but the world is more excited when he meets Sharon Stone.

And so a serious spiritual leader is treated as a pop star, and a doctor of metaphysics is sought out by everyone, from every culture, who has a problem in his life. As a monk, he seems more than happy to offer what he can, as much as he can, but none of it helps him towards the liberation of his people. I ask him one day about how Tibet is likely to be compromised by its

SUN AFTER DARK

complicity with the mass media, and he looks back at me
shrewdly, and with a penetrating gaze. "If there are people who
use Tibetans or the Tibetan situation for their own purposes," he
says, "or if they associate with some publicity for their own bene-
fit, there's very little we can do. But the important thing is for us
not to be involved in this publicity, or associate with these people
for our own interests."

The razor-sharp reasoning is typical, even if it doesn't quite
address the conundrum in which he finds himself. For precisely
in order to satisfy his inner and outer mandate, the Dalai Lama is
obliged to traffic in the world incessantly. He has to listen to a
reporter asking him how he'd like to be remembered—which is,
in the Buddhist context, akin to asking the Pope what he thinks
of Jennifer Lopez. ("I really lost my temper," he tells me, of the
question, "though I didn't show it.") He has to answer for every
scandal that touches any of the many, often highly suspect
Tibetans and Tibetan groups around the world. And he has to
endure and address every controversy that arises when his image
is used by Apple Computer, or when younger Tibetans deride
him as an out-of-it peacenik who's done nothing to help Tibet
for forty years.

As we spoke for day after day in the radiant fall afternoons,
young monks practicing ritual debating outside his front door,
the snowcaps shining in the distance, and the hopes of Tibet
poignantly, palpably in the air around the ragged town of exiles,
the time the Dalai Lama most lit up, in some respects, was when
he spoke of some Catholic monks he'd run into in France who
live in complete isolation for years on end and "remain almost
like prisoners" as they meditate. "Wonderful!" he pronounced,
leaving it to his visitor to deduce that, left to his own devices,
that's how he'd like to be.

At this point, after two Dalai Lama autobiographies and two major Hollywood films telling the story of his life, the other-worldly contours of the Dalai Lama's life are well known: his birth in a cowshed in rural Tibet, in what was locally known as the Wood Hog Year (1935); his discovery by a search party of monks, who'd been led to him by a vision in a sacred lake; the tests administered to a two-year-old who, mysteriously, greeted the monks from far-off Lhasa as their leader, and in their distant dialect. Yet what the mixture of folktale and Shakespearean drama doesn't always catch is that the single dominant theme of his life, a Buddhist might say, is loss.

To someone who reads the world in terms of temporal glory, it's a stirring story of a four-year-old peasant boy ascending the Lion Throne to rule one of the most exotic treasures on earth. To someone who really lives the philosophy for which the Dalai Lama stands, it could play out in a different key. At two, he lost the peace of his quiet life in a wood-and-stone house where he slept in the kitchen. At four he lost his home, and his freedom to be a regular person, when he was pronounced head of state. Soon thereafter, he lost something of his family, too, and most of his ties with the world at large, as he embarked on a formidable sixteen-year course of monastic studies, and was forced, at the age of six, to choose a regent.

The Dalai Lama has written with typical warmth about his otherworldly boyhood in the cold, thousand-roomed Potala Palace, where he played games with the palace sweepers, rigged up a hand-cranked projector on which he could watch Tarzan movies and *Henry V,* and clobbered his only real playmate—his immediate elder brother Lobsang Samten—in the knowledge that no one would be quick to punish a boy regarded as an incarnation of the god of compassion (and a king to boot). Yet the overwhelming feature of his childhood was its loneliness. Often, he recalls, he would go out onto the rooftop of his palace and watch the other little boys of Lhasa playing in the street. Every time his brother left, he recalls standing "at the window, watching, my heart full of sorrow as he disappeared into the distance."

The Dalai Lama has never pretended that he does not have a human side, and though it is that side that exults in everything that comes his way, it is also that side that cannot fail to grieve at times. When the Chinese, newly united by Mao Zedong, attacked Tibet's eastern frontiers in 1950, the fifteen-year-old boy was forced hurriedly to take over the temporal as well as the spiritual leadership of his country, and so lost his boyhood (if not his innocence), and his last vestiges of freedom. In his teens he was traveling to Beijing, overriding the wishes of his fearful people, to negotiate with Mao and Zhou En-lai, and not long thereafter he became only the second Dalai Lama to leave Tibet, when it seemed his life might be in peril.

At twenty-four, a few days after he completed his doctoral studies, and shone in an oral in front of thousands of appraising monks, he lost his home for good: the "Wish-Fulfilling Gem," as he is known to Tibetans, had to dress up as a soldier and flee across the highest mountains on earth, dodging Chinese planes, and seated on a hybrid yak. The drama of that loss lives inside him still. I asked him one sunny afternoon about the saddest moment in his life, and he told me that he was moved to tears usually only when he talked of Buddha, or thought of compassion—or heard, as he sometimes does every day, the stories and appeals of the terrified refugees who've stolen out of Tibet to come and see him.

Generally, he said, in his firm, prudent way, "sadness, I think, is comparatively manageable." But before he said any of that, he looked into the distance and recalled: "I left the Norbulingka Palace that late night, and some of my close friends and one dog I left behind. Then, just when I was crossing the border into India, I remember my final farewell, mainly to my bodyguards. They were deliberately facing the Chinese, and when they made farewell with me, they were determined to return. So that means"—his eyes were close to misting over—"they were facing death, or something like that." In the thirty-nine years since then, he's never seen the land he was born to rule.

I, too, remember that drama: the fairy-tale flight of the boyking from the Forbidden Kingdom was the first world event that made an impression on me when I was growing up; a little later, when my father went to India to greet the newly arrived Tibetan, he came back with a picture of the monk as a little boy, which the Dalai Lama gave him when he talked of his three-year-old in Oxford. Since then, like many of us, I've run into the Tibetan leader everywhere I go—at Harvard, in New York, in the hills of Malibu, in Japan—and have had the even stranger experience of seeing him somehow infiltrate the most unlikely worlds: my graduate-school professor of Virginia Woolf suddenly came into my life again as editor of a book of the Dalai Lama's talks about the Gospels; at the Olympics, a longtime friend and sportswriter for the *New York Times* started reminiscing about how he covered the Dalai Lama on the Tibetan's first U.S. tour, in 1979, and found him great because he was so humble. "It sounds like he considers you part of the family," a friend once said, when I told her that the Dalai Lama and his equally mischievous younger brother call me "Pinocchio." But really, his gift is for regarding all of the world as part of his family.

At the same time, the world itself has not always been very interested in the details of his faraway country, or of a tradition that seems to belong to another world. When Tibet appealed for help against China to the newly formed United Nations, it was Britain and India, its two ostensible sponsors, who argued against even hearing the motion. And as recently as the 1980s, I remember, the Dalai Lama's press conferences in New York were almost deserted; when once I organized a lunch for him with a group of editors, one of them phoned a couple of days before to call it off, because no one really wanted to come into the office on a Monday just to chat with a Tibetan monk. When first I visited him in Dharamsala, in 1974, I really did feel as if I were looking in on one of the deposed emperors of China or Vietnam, sitting in a far-off exile. As we sat drinking tea in his modest, colorful cottage, clouds passed through the room from the rains out-side—all we could see through the large windows was mist and grey—and it seemed as if we were truly sitting in the heavens, at least a mile above anything that felt real.

Yet one of the paradoxes of the Dalai Lama's life—a paradox to answer the koan that has been his fulfillment of a spiritual duty in the world—is that it was, it seems, his monastic training that allowed him to be so focused and charismatic a presence in the world. In his early years in India, the Dalai Lama used the world's neglect of him to organize his exiled community and to write his country's constitution (in part to allow for his own impeachment). Even exile could be a liberation, he was saying (and showing his compatriots): it freed him from the age-old protocol that so shackled him in Tibet and it brought the forever feuding groups of Tibet together in a common cause. Most of all, though, he used his free time to go on long meditation retreats, enjoying a solitude that could never have been his in Tibet (or can be, now, in Dharamsala).

Robert Thurman, the professor of Tibetan studies at Columbia (and father of actress Uma), remembers first meeting the Dalai Lama in 1964, when he, full of spiritual ambitions, cross-questioned the young Tibetan about *shunyata*, or voidness, while the Dalai Lama questioned him, no less eagerly, about Freud and the American bicameral system. "It was fun," Thurman says, using the word people often use of the Dalai Lama. "We were young together." At the same time, the answers that the monk only in his twenties then gave to complex theological questions were less good, Thurman feels, than those offered by more senior monks.

When the Tibetan leader emerged from his retreats, though, and came out into the world—Thurman saw him on his first U.S. tour, in 1979—"I almost keeled over. His personal warmth and magnetism were so strong. In the past, of course, he had the ritual charisma of being the Dalai Lama, and he's always been charming and interesting and very witty. But now he'd opened up some inner wellspring of energy and attention and intelligence. He was glorious."

And yet that air of responsibility—the word he always stresses in the same breath as "compassion"—has never left him. I remember going to see him the day after he won the Nobel Prize, when he happened to be staying (as is so typical of his life) in a suburban ranch house in Newport Beach. What struck me at the time was that, as soon as he saw me, he whisked me (as he would no doubt have whisked any visitor) into a little room, and spent his first few minutes looking for a chair in which I would be comfortable—as if I were the new Nobel laureate and he the intrusive journalist.

But what I also remember from that moment was that, even as the world was feting him—congratulatory telegrams and faxes pouring into the rec room downstairs—he couldn't let himself off the hook. "Sometimes," he confessed, "I wonder whether my efforts really have an effect. I sometimes feel that unless there is a bigger movement, the bigger issues will not change. But how to start this bigger movement? Originally, it must come from individual initiative."

The only way, he concluded, was through "constant effort, tireless effort, pursuing clear goals with sincere effort." Every time he left a room, he said, he tried to switch off the light. "In a way, it's silly. But if another person follows my example, then a hundred persons, there is an effect. It is the only way. The bigger nations and more powerful leaders are not taking care. So we poor human beings must make the effort."

Meeting him now, I find him a lot more businesslike than he was in those days (and, of course, much more fluent in English); when TV crews come to interview him, he knows how to advise them on where to set up their cameras (and when we begin talking, he is quick to point out that my tape recorder is moving suspiciously fast). He's not less jolly than before, perhaps, but he does seem more determined to speak from the serious side of himself, as the years go on, and Tibet draws ever closer to oblivion. Where he used to greet me with an Indian *namaste*, now he does so with a handshake, though the Dalai Lama does not so much shake your hand as rub it within his own, as if to impart to it some of his warmth.

As we talk, though—every afternoon at two, for day after day—he takes off his glasses and rubs his eyes; his aides say that in recent years, for the first time ever, they've seen him exhausted, his head slumped back in his chair (this the man usually seen leaning into the conversation, as if to bring to it all his attention and beady-eyed vigor). He doesn't have much time for spiritual practice now, he tells me—only four hours a day (his duties increasing as he becomes a more senior monk). He still likes to do "some repair work, of watches and small instruments," and he still loves tending to his flowers. One of the longest and most animated answers he gives me comes when I ask after his "four small cats." But these days the only real break he can take comes in listening to the BBC World Service, to which he cheerfully confesses himself addicted.

This is the tendency of an engaging, still-boyish character alight with curiosity; but it's also the confession of a man whose duties are almost entirely tied up with the dealings of the world, on a minute-by-minute level. One thing the Dalai Lama is not is otherworldly. He can explain in precise detail why the Tibetan cause is weaker than that of the Palestinians, or how globalism is, at its best, advancing a kind of Buddhism in *mufti*. His references nearly always come from the day's most recent news, and he watches everything—from the fall of the Berlin Wall to the tragedy of Rwanda—both to see how it illuminates some metaphysical theory and to see what other kind of teaching it can impart. Exile has allowed him, he will tell you, to become a student of the world in a way that no earlier Dalai Lama could, and to see a planet that previously he, and the Dalai Lamas before him, could glimpse only through the parted curtains of a palanquin. The best aspect of his traveling is that he can schedule meetings with scientists and psychologists and Hopi leaders, all of whom, he believes, can help him refine his understanding of his own tradition. Buddhists can and should learn from Catholics, from physicists, even from Communists, he is quick to tell his startled followers—and if the words of the Buddha (let alone of the Dalai Lama) are not borne out by the evidence, they must be discarded instantly.

This is one reason why he seems much more interested in

asking questions than in giving answers, and much more comfortable as a student (which he's been, in the context of Tibetan Buddhism, most of his life) than as a teacher. It is also why I would say his sovereign quality is alertness: watch the Dalai Lama enter a crowded auditorium, or sit through a long monastic ceremony that has many others nodding off, and you will notice him looking around keenly for what he can pick up: a friend to whom he can unself-consciously wave, some little detail that will bring a smile to his face. Alertness is the place where the slightly impish boy and the rigorously trained monk converge, and though the world at large most responds to his heart—the pleasure afforded by his beam and air of kindness and good nature—the specific core of him comes no less from his mind, and the analytical faculties honed in one of the world's most sophisticated metaphysical technologies. It's not unusual, I've come to see by now, for the Dalai Lama to remember a sentence he's delivered to you seven years before, or to complete an answer he began ninety minutes ago, while lacing up his sturdy mountain boots. Sometimes, in large gatherings, he will pick out a face he last saw in Lhasa forty years before. Once, as we were talking, he suddenly remembered something an Englishman had said to him twenty years before—about the value of sometimes saying "I don't know"—and asked me, searchingly, what I thought of it.

Again, the irony here is that the mindfulness he's cultivated in meditation—on retreats, and at the hands of pitilessly strict teachers—is what has helped him in his travels; spiritual training—this is one of the lessons of his life and his example—has constant practical application in the world. Much of the time he's speaking to people who know nothing about Buddhism—who may even be hostile to it—and he's mastered the art of speaking simply, and ecumenically, from the heart, stressing, as he does, "spirituality without faith—simply being a good human being, a warm-hearted person, a person with a sense of responsibility." Talking to his monks, he delivers philosophical lectures that few of the rest of us could begin to follow; speaking to the world, he realizes that the most important thing is not to run before you can walk. The title of a typical book of his mentions not "enlightening" the heart but, simply, "lightening" it.

In a sense, he's turned his predicament to advantage in part by learning about Western religions, and meditation practices in other traditions, as earlier Dalai Lamas could seldom do. And he's also had to deal with a worldwide stampede towards a Buddhism for which the world may not be ready (to such a point that, more and more as the years go on, he tells Westerners not to become Buddhists, but just to stick to their own tradition, where there's less danger of mixed motives, and certainly less likelihood of confusion). Listening to him speak everywhere from São Paulo to Chicago, Philip Glass says: "The word 'Buddha' never came up. He talks about compassion, he talks about right living. And it's very powerful and persuasive to people because it's clear he's not there to convert them."

Pragmatism, in short, trumps dogmatism. And logic defers to nothing. "Out of 5.7 million people," he tells me one day, his eyes glittering with the delight of a student immersed in one of Tibet's ritual debates, "the majority of them are certainly not believers. We can't argue with them, tell them they should be believers. No! Impossible! And, realistically speaking, if the majority of humanity remains nonbelievers, it doesn't matter. No problem! The problem is that the majority have lost, or ignore, the deeper human values—compassion, a sense of responsibility. That is our big concern. For whenever there is a society or community without deeper human values, then even one single human family cannot be a happy family."

Then—and it isn't hard to see the still-eager student playing his winning card—he goes on: "Even animals, from a Buddhist viewpoint, also have the potential of showing affection towards their own children, or their own babies—and also towards us. Dogs, cats, if we treat them nicely, openly, trustingly, they also respond. But without religion; they have no faith!" Therefore, he says triumphantly, kindness is more fundamental than belief.

Yet the deepest loss of all in the Dalai Lama's often bright and blessing-filled life is that all the friends he's made worldwide, all the presidents and prime ministers he's won over, all the analytical reasoning with which he argues for compassion and responsibility have not really helped him at all in what is the main endeavor of his life: safeguarding the people of Tibet, and sustaining a Tibetan identity among a scattered population, six million of whom have not seen their leader for two generations, and the other 140,000 of whom have not, in many cases, seen their homeland. Many of those who see him flying across five continents in a year (in business class) and delivering lectures to sold-out halls don't realize that he's working with a staff drawn from a population smaller than that of Warren, Michigan, and with a circle of advisors who'd never seen the world, or known much about it, before they were propelled into exile.

Within the Tibetan community, he remains as lonely as ever, I think. His people still regard him, quite literally, as a god, with the result that even young Indian-born Tibetans who are fluent in English are too shy to offer their services as translators. And as fast as he tries to push democracy onto his people—urging them to contradict him and to make their own plans regardless of him—they push autocracy back onto him: most Tibetans believe everything the Dalai Lama says, except when he says that the

Dalai Lama is fallible. None of this has been made easier by the fact that he is clearly his country's main selling point, so that it can seem as if the destiny of a whole people rests on the shoulders of one decidedly mortal man.

Thus he's obviously grateful for the chance to meet foreigners, who will more readily challenge and counsel him—even criticize him—and he's lucky to have a large and unusually gifted family around him, two of whose members are incarnated lamas themselves. His younger brother Tenzin Choegyal lives down the road, and even as the Dalai Lama claims to be unconcerned about all the complications that arise as Tibet and Tibetan Buddhism go around the world, his kid brother (who shed the monastic robes into which he was born) is outspoken in calling the situation "a hell of a hodgepodge," and referring to the West's infatuation with Tibet, and the Tibetans who make corrupt use of that, as "the Shangri-La syndrome."

Even for those who understand it, after all, Tibetan Buddhism is a vividly charged and esoteric body of teachings, a "unique blend," as the British judge and Buddhist scholar Christmas Humphreys once wrote, "of the noblest Buddhist principles and debased sorcery." Its core, as with all Buddhism, is a belief in suffering and emptiness, and the need for compassion in the face of those. But unlike the stripped-down austerities of Zen, say, it swarms with animist spirits, pictures of copulating deities, and Tantric practices of sexuality and magic that, in the wrong hands, or without the proper training, can be inflammable.

The Dalai Lama's very equanimity and his refusal to be autocratic (even if he had the time) have left him relatively powerless as all kinds of questionable things are done in the name of his philosophy. Unlike their Catholic counterparts, he says, Tibetan and Buddhist groups "have no central authority. They're all quite independent." To top things off, three-hundred-year-old rivalries that used to be conducted in the privacy of the Himalaya are now played out on the world's front pages.

Five years ago, with no help from the Chinese, an unseemly mess broke out when two six-year-old boys were presented as the new incarnation of the high Karmapa lineage, one of them endorsed by the Dalai Lama, the other by friends of the departed lama's family. One of the most prominent lamas in the West was banned from entering America for many years after a $10 million sexual harassment suit was brought against him; perhaps the most famous rinpoche in the West was notorious for his women, his drinking, and his brutal bodyguards, and left a community riddled with AIDS. Not long ago, three members of the Dalai Lama's inner circle were found murdered in their beds, the victims, it was supposed, of some complex internecine rivalry.

The Dalai Lama takes all this in stride—he was putting down insurrections at the age of eleven, after all—but the whole issue of authority (when to enforce it, and how to delegate it) takes on a special urgency as he moves towards his seventies. The finding of a new Dalai Lama when all of Tibet is in Chinese hands would in the best of circumstances be treacherous; it became doubly so three years ago when Beijing unilaterally hijacked the second-highest incarnation in Tibet, that of the Panchen Lama, placing the Dalai Lama's six-year-old choice under house arrest and installing a candidate of its own. (The Panchen Lama, by tradition, is the figure officially responsible for authorizing the Dalai Lama's own incarnation, and the maneuver suggested that the Chinese may have few qualms about coming up with their own puppet as the next Dalai Lama.)

In response to this, the Dalai Lama has been typically canny. More than a decade ago, he reminds me, he said, "If I die in the near future, and the Tibetan people want another reincarnation, a Fifteenth Dalai Lama, while we are still outside Tibet, my

reincarnation will definitely appear outside Tibet. Because"—
the logic, as ever, is impeccable—"the very purpose of the incarnation is to fulfill the work that has been started by the previous
life." So, he goes on, "the reincarnation of the Fourteenth Dalai
Lama, logically, will not be a reincarnation which disturbs, or is
an obstacle to, that work. Quite clear, isn't it?" In any case, he says
cheerfully, "at a certain stage the Dalai Lama institution will disappear. That does not mean that Tibetan Buddhism will cease.
But the incarnation comes and goes, comes and goes."

As ever, few of his supporters are equally ready to acquiesce
in such lèse-majesté (when I ask a group of Tibetan officials if
this one will be the last Dalai Lama, they all say anxiously, "No,
no"). And many of them, too, have found it hard to countenance
his policy of forgiving the Chinese (he has referred to Mao as
"remarkable," called himself "half-Marxist, half-Buddhist," and
stepped back from his original demands of independence to calling only for an autonomous "Zone of Peace"). The pressure on
him to forswear his policy of nonviolence has intensified as the
years go by, and Chinese repression comes ever closer to render-
ing Tibet extinct.

"In one way, yes," he tells me, "my position has become
weaker, because there's been no development, no progress. In
spite of my open approach, of maximum concessions, the Chinese position becomes even harder and harder." Last year, all
photographs of the exiled leader were banned in Tibet, and
monks and nuns continue to be imprisoned and tortured at will,
in what the International Commission of Jurists long ago called
a policy of genocide. Yet the Dalai Lama takes heart from the
fact that more and more Chinese individuals have been speaking
out for Tibet (as they would not have done, he feels, if he'd been
more militant); not long ago, he gave a special three-day initia-
tion in Los Angeles expressly for those of Chinese descent.

"To isolate China is totally wrong," he tells me forcefully. "China needs the outside world, and the outside world needs China." Besides, even China stands to gain from a freer Tibet. "If the Tibetan issue can be resolved through dialogue, and if we remain happily in the People's Republic of China, it will have immense impact in the minds of another six million Chinese in Hong Kong and, eventually, twenty-one million Chinese in Taiwan. The image of China in the whole world will, overnight, change."

That is the position he must take, of course, and a skeptic would say, confronted with his stubborn optimism, that it can be a little perverse to celebrate clouds just because they show us silver linings. Yet it's worth recalling that the Dalai Lama's policy of forgiveness is not an abstract thing. When he speaks of suffering, it's as one who has seen his land destroyed, up to 1.2 million of his people killed, and all but 13 of his 6,254 monasteries laid waste. When he talks of inner peace, it's as one who was away on the road, struggling for his cause, when his mother, his senior tutor, and his only childhood playmate, Lobsang Samten, died. And when he speaks of forbearance, it's as one who is still publicly called by Beijing a "wolf in monk's robes."

As I left Dharamsala, in fact—at dawn, with the Dalai Lama leading his monks in a three-hour ceremony while the sun came up—it struck me that the man has lived out a kind of archetypal destiny of our times: a boy born in a peasant village in a world that had scarcely seen a wheel has ended up confronting the great forces of the day, exile, global travel, and, especially, the mass media; and a man from a culture we associate with Shangri-La now faces machine guns on the one hand, and a Lhasa Holiday Inn on the other, while J. Peterman catalogues crow, "Crystals are out! Tibetan Buddhism is in!" It says much about the challenges of the moment that a spokesman for an ancient, highly complex philosophy finds himself in rock-concert arenas obliged to answer questions about abortion and the "patriarchal" nature of Tibetan Buddhism.

Yet to these twenty-first-century conundrums, the Dalai Lama is aiming to bring a state-of-the-art solution. Tibet's predicament, he tells me with practiced fluency, is not just about a faraway culture hidden behind snowcaps five miles high. It's about ecology, since the Ganges, Brahmaputra, Mekong, and Yellow Rivers all have their sources in Tibet. It's about natural resources, since, "according to Chinese official documents, there are more than one hundred sixty-six or one hundred sixty-seven different minerals in Tibet." It's about human rights, and a unique and imperiled culture, and a buffer zone "between these two giants, India and China."

Most of all, it's about a different way of moving through the world. Far from turning his back on the strangeness of the times, the Dalai Lama is taking it on wholeheartedly, to the point of working with forces that many of us might see as compromised. ("We're just fallen sentient beings," Richard Gere says, touchingly, of the Hollywood community. "We need some help, too.") If part of the Dalai Lama is suggesting that monks can't afford to be unworldly hermits, another part is suggesting that politicians need not be aggressive schemers. Compassion, he argues over and over, only stands to reason.

If the Dalai Lama were a dreamer, it would be easy to write him off. In fact, he's an attentive, grounded, empirical soul whose optimism has only been bolstered by the breakthroughs achieved by his friends Desmond Tutu and Václav Havel. Havel, indeed, who became the first head of state to recognize the Dalai Lama, within thirteen hours of coming to power, has been a powerful spokesman for this new kind of statesmanship. The politician of conscience, the Czech leader writes, need not have a graduate degree in political science, or years of training in duplicity. Instead, he may rely on "qualities like fellow-feeling, the ability to talk to others, insight, the capacity to grasp quickly not only problems but also human character, the ability to make contact, a sense of moderation." In all those respects, the Czech president might well have been thinking of a canny Tibetan scientist with a surprising gift for repairing old watches, tending to sick parrots, and, as it happens, making broken things whole once again.

1998

HAPPY
HOUR
IN
THE
HEART
OF
DARKNESS

For almost twenty years now, Tuol Sleng has been a notorious memorial to the Khmer Rouge killers who ruled Cambodia from 1975 to 1979. Bump down a potholed backstreet in the capital of Phnom Penh, and you come upon a former girls' school bare except for the rusted beds on which Pol Pot's men interrogated victims, and the U.S. munitions cans they used as toilets. Display cases are littered with the hoes and shovels and iron staves they used to beat people to death; along the walls hundreds upon hundreds of black-and-white faces stare back at you, dazed or terrified, recalling the people, often children, and often themselves Khmer Rouge executioners, who were executed here. One large wall is dominated by a map of Cambodia made up entirely of skulls.

Outside, in rough letters, the regulations of the place are written out by hand, in English and Cambodian—"While getting lashes and electrification, you must not cry at all." Step out into the sun, and cripples swarm around you, crying, "Sir, I have no money to buy rice. Sir?"

The "Museum of Genocidal Crime," as the road signs call it, has long been one of the principal tourist sights in Phnom Penh, long enough for locals to have stubbed out cigarettes in the eyes of Pol Pot in one photograph. But a little while ago, the currency of the torture center changed when the man who had overseen it for four years, Kang Khek Ieu, generally known as "Duch," was suddenly discovered, by foreign journalists, in a western village. He was running a crushed-ice stall in the countryside and had certificates of baptism to prove his status as a born-again Christian. The man who oversaw the execution of at least sixteen thousand of his countrymen had papers from American churches testifying to his "personal leadership" and "team-building skills."

Like many of his Khmer Rouge comrades, Duch, now fifty-six, had been a teacher (educated, as it happens, in U.S. A.I.D. schools); unlike them, he admitted that he had done "very bad things" in his life. More recently, he claimed, he had been working for international relief organizations, helping out in local camps. "He was our best worker," said a refugee official when told that the man who had tried to protect children from typhoid was the notorious torturer who had once written *Kill them all* over lists of nine-year-olds.

Such black ironies are still much too common everywhere you turn in this bleeding, often broken country where every moral certainty was exiled long ago, and a visitor finds himself in a labyrinth of sorts, every path leading to a cul-de-sac. On paper at least, this is a time of hope for ill-starred Cambodia. In 1998

Pol Pot finally died in his jungle hideout, and just before the new year, two of the last three Khmer Rouge leaders, Khieu Samphan and Nuon Chea, turned themselves in to the government of Hun Sen. The last Khmer Rouge bigwig still at large, Ta Mok, a one-legged general known as "the Butcher," was captured in March, and now (alone among them) awaits trial. For the first time in more than a generation, there are no Cambodians in refugee camps across the border in Thailand, and the Khmer Rouge, held responsible for the deaths of 1.7 million Cambodians during their four years in power alone, are silent.

Yet every prospect of new sunlight in Cambodia brings new shadows, and justice itself seems a rusty chain that will only bloody anyone who tries to touch it. To try the Khmer Rouge chieftains would be, in a sense, to prosecute the whole country: almost everyone around—from the exiled King Sihanouk to the one-eyed prime minister to the man next door—has some connection to the Khmer Rouge killers. And even those who don't have come to strange accommodations: the local lawyer who agreed to represent Ta Mok lost his own wife and twelve-year-old daughter to his client's comrades. "So many people killed many people," says a young Cambodian in the western town of Siem Reap. "Even my uncle, he killed many people. That is how my father was safe. So we say, 'If you kill Khmer Rouge, you must kill everyone.'"

To pursue the old men who committed their worst crimes twenty years ago is to risk setting new furies into motion, the government protests, and to perpetuate the cycle of violence when already forty thousand Cambodians are limbless and more than 50 percent of the country's children are stunted. Yet to turn over a new page and let bygones be bygones is to leave justice itself as broken and legless as the Buddhas in the National Museum. Almost certainly, the government will try to stage enough of a trial to satisfy the international community, on which it depends for funds, while disrupting as little as possible.

Even the sudden death of Pol Pot left a hollowness in many Cambodian hearts: the man who obliterated the country, its society, and its fields, died, without explanation, just as there was hope of trying him. "I don't want to think more about Khmer Rouge," says Keo Lundi, a gaunt, sad-eyed thirty-nine-year-old who shows visitors around the blood-stained floors of Tuol Sleng. "I don't want to know that Duch dies." He bangs his hand against a rusted post. "They killed my brother. They pulled down my life. They took my education—everything—to zero. I want peace."

The prospects for that are better now than they have been for many years: the main war visible in Phnom Penh is between five rival "hand-phone" companies fighting for the loyalties of ubiquitous cell-phone addicts, and a few weeks ago the country was finally admitted to the Southeast Asian economic community, ASEAN. Women who would otherwise be pushed towards prostitution are now employed in huge numbers—135,000 of them in all—in 165 government factories, and tourists, for the first time in thirty years, can fly directly to the great temples of Angkor, bringing money to the country's empty coffers. Yet the suspicion remains that peace can be acquired only at the expense of justice. To embrace the future, it seems, is to evade the past.

It is a curious thing these days to wander around Phnom Penh, a city of potholes and puddles where most of the elegant French colonial buildings behind gates look like haunted houses taken over by squatters too concerned with their survival tomorrow to worry about upkeep today. Side streets are piled high with rotting garbage, and the small handmade signs above the open sewers say things like SAVING AIDS AND MADMAN VICTIM ASSOCIATION. Policemen crouch on the sidewalks, playing tic-tac-toe in the cracks of the pavement, and the fanciest hotel in town shuts its gates every night as if to keep the jungle and the darkness at bay.

The potholes extend psychically, too: almost every Cambodian you talk to has huge gaps in his life story, long silences. Since Pol Pot eliminated all those with education or knowledge of the outside world, Phnom Penh became a city of country people, as well as of orphans, and you still will not find doctors or teachers or lawyers of a certain age. No one knows what their neighbors suffered, or how exactly they survived. To survive today, school-age girls sell themselves for two dollars a visit—ignoring what may be the fastest-rising AIDS infection rate in the world—and children scramble in the dust for foreigners' coins long after midnight. Their faces, you can't help but notice, are the same as the ones in the torture center.

Amidst all the dilapidation, there are gaudy, anomalous explosions of affluence—huge, multistory palaces offering KARAOKE MASSAGE in neon letters, and ads in the local paper for Harry Winston jewels. Above the Mekong a grand casino posts notices about what you must do if you have $3,500 in cash, and the minimum bet at many tables is $20. The security guards who frisk you—NO KNIFE OR OFFENSIVE, say the signs, NO MILITARY/POLICE UNIFORM UNLESS ON OFFICIAL VISIT—wear yellow smiley buttons.

Much of the money comes, of course, from overseas investors eager to make a killing out of need, and gambling that the economy can only improve. "This is the first time since I came here in 1992 when I can feel truly confident of making a profit," says a Singaporean businessman, sipping pumpkin soup with gold leaf in it (in a hotel where even the telephone receivers are scented with jasmine). The appetizer alone costs as much as a local judge (generally uneducated) earns in maybe six months.

Along the broad streets—still called Quai Karl Marx and Mao Tse Tung and Yugoslavie on many of the maps—there are clusters of Irish pubs and new French cafés, "Little Tokyo" restaurants and Filipino drinking-places. Local boys in fezzes sit outside a new Turkish restaurant along the Mekong, and the Royal Palace—almost too fittingly—stands where Lenin Boulevard meets "English Street" (so nicknamed for all the English classes on offer). Outside the latest cybercafé, urchins in wheelchairs swivel around at foreigners, crying, "No have mother!"

For a certain kind of foreigner, there is a half-illicit thrill in living in a place where the officials are running drugs and girls and antique Buddhas when the guerrillas are not. At night, in the Heart of Darkness bar, the talk is all of $200 hit men and whole villages in the business of peddling thirteen-year-old girls. Pizza restaurants are called "Happy" and "Ecstatic" in honor of their ganja toppings, and two of the main sites of entertainment are shooting ranges (public and private) where you can lob hand grenades or fire away with M-16 assault rifles. To rent a twenty-four-room guest house on a lake, with a view of distant temples, costs $425 a month.

"I lived for two years without electricity," says a South American restaurant owner, sitting at a café while a woman crouches at her feet, giving her toenails their weekly polish. "Only by candle. It cost me two dollars a week." Wander off the main streets and you are in a maze of little lanes—completely unlit and unpaved—where a former Zen monk runs a guest house and Africans on the run live by teaching English.

In such places Cambodia has the air of a society with no laws where some protective coating, some layer of civilization keeping Darwin's jungle remote, has been torn away. The local paper reads like it was written by a Jacobean playwright with a taste for black irony. A motorist crashes into the Independence Monument, it says, the seventh such fatality this year. More than twelve thousand "ghost soldiers"—nonexistent employees—have been found on the Ministry of Defense payrolls. A Frenchman here to help Cambodia is charged with running a brothel full of underage boys.

It seems almost apt that half the cars you see have steering wheels on the left and half have them on the right, ensuring bloody accidents every day.

In the midst of all this, the ones who live among ghosts conduct their own private investigations. "My friends think I'm crazy," says a well-to-do Cambodian who returned here from Canada. "People tell me, 'Why do you want to look at these things? It's easier to forget.' But I want to understand why it happened"—he means the self-extermination of his country—"so it will never happen again." When Pol Pot died, Keo Lundi, from the Tuol Sleng center, says, "I spent my own money to go to his province, to talk to his brother and sister. I wanted to know what he was like as a child." What he found was that Pol Pot—born Saloth Sar—was a notably mild-mannered boy, pious and delicate, who "never played with a gun" and often accompanied his mother to the pagoda. His own siblings claim not to have known that it was their courteous brother who was "Brother Number One," the man who loosed a national madness.

The hope now is that Duch, the last Khmer Rouge leader to leave the city when the country's longtime enemies, the Vietnamese, took over in January 1979, may shed some light on what happened. But though the government has, for the time being, acceded to the demands of the world, and the U.N., to hold a partly international tribunal of the Khmer Rouge leaders, almost everyone agrees that terms like "justice" and "democracy" are virtual luxuries in a country as desperate as Cambodia, where politics can often look like a Swiss bank account under a false name.

"I don't want to watch the trials," a diplomat in a Western embassy says with feeling. "Because everything that has happened in the past year has been staged. So we know already what will happen. They will blame everything on Pol Pot, on others who are gone. Or on the Americans. Or the King. It will be lies."

On New Year's Day, as a visitor inspects carvings of demons and gods and mythological battles at the haunted temple of Angkor Wat, suddenly a Cambodian standing nearby clutches a pillar till his knuckles turn white. "Look," he says, swallowing. "There's Khieu Samphan!" He points to a trim elderly man in white shirt and slacks, walking with relatively little protection towards his helicopter. "He killed so many," says the visitor. "He killed my mother, my father," says the man, who was himself forced out of his home as a boy to work in the fields. Khieu and Nuon Chea are walking through a city they have orphaned, among people whose lives they have destroyed, VIP sight-seers (courtesy of the government) this bright festival day.

"Let us finish the war," says a twenty-five-year-old local nearby, flush with the promise of a new future. "We are Buddhists: if you do badly, bad will come to you. Let us shake hands."

Six months later, the debate continues like a tolling bell. On the twenty-third anniversary of Pol Pot's announcement of national collectivization, a thousand or so people gather at dawn in the killing fields, among 129 mass graves, some of them reserved for women and children, some for 166 corpses found without heads. For years the rite was known as the "Day of Hate." Now, in more hopeful times, it is called the "Day of Memory."

1999

DEAD

MAN

WALKING

The classic travel writer takes us on a quest, even if he doesn't know exactly what he's after; with the haunted German wanderer W. G. Sebald, the dominant impression is always that of flight. A flight from the past, and from all that he has suffered there; but also—agonizingly—a flight into the past, since everywhere he goes, whatever he sees, and whomever he meets reflect back to him precisely the world he's trying to put behind him. There's no escape. With the classic traveler we generally feel that we're being taken by the hand and led out into the world; with Sebald (so uneasy he can't even acknowledge to us that his journeys are a fact, nonfiction), we are always looking back even as we move forward, like cursed figures from an ancient myth.

You get a sense of this predicament—flight not as liberation, but as compulsion—as soon as you pick up the latest of his books to be translated into English. The dust jacket of *Vertigo*, at least in the British edition, tells you, not very helpfully, that it belongs to the genre of "Fiction/Travel/History." The table of contents, even in translation, offers two sections, out of four, with Italian titles. The author refuses to give us his first name, in the style that now seems archaic, and his alter-ego narrator will check into a hotel room under a name not his own. Sebald has lived in England for more than thirty years—teaching literature, no less—and yet he chooses to write still in his native German.

Clearly, you gather, his sense of identity is slippery and his theme, at some level, is all the things he cannot speak about (he was born, the book's cover tells you, in Germany, in 1944). And as soon as you open the cover and fall into his restless nightmare of a journey, you find you are moving with no hope of orientation or forward motion. There is no sense of home around you in his world, no sense of family, or community, no sense, even, of a settled reality. By page 4 you are being introduced to weird drawings of "horses that plunged off the track in a frenzy of fear" during Napoleon's Italian campaign in 1800; by page 5 you are moving into a "light that is already fading." The thrust of the opening section is that nothing is what it seems: most of what the "perennial traveler" Stendhal remembered about the Napoleonic campaign he accompanied never happened.

Then the curtain rises on the second section of the book, and the never-changing Sebald narrator, the author's double in a sense, comes out from the wings and takes us into the voice, the theme—the world—that are fast coming to seem Sebaldian: "In October 1980 I traveled from England, where I had been living for nearly twenty-five years in a county that was almost always under grey skies, to Vienna, hoping that a change of place would help me get over a particularly difficult period in my life."

Though *Vertigo* is the third of Sebald's books to be translated into English, it is the first of them to have been written, and so lays out the foundations for what increasingly seems to be one long, lifetime's work that could be called *À la Fuite de Temps Perdu*. In all these works, a narrator, in all ways indistinguishable from the author, takes off on long, unsettled wanderings, in pursuit of some riddle that will not leave him alone. He mixes up his travels with portraits of other enigmatic wanderers and misfits, and the text is broken up at regular, irregular intervals with cryptic photographs, copies of receipts from trains or restaurants, maps taken from old books. Uncaptioned, and bearing only the most oblique relation to the text around them, the scraps serve only to intensify the sense of placelessness and silence.

There are few other beings in this desolate, black-and-white world, and those we meet are as disconnected as the narrator: solitary eccentrics lost in their own obsessions, sad outcasts set aside as mad. We see coffins, hear tolling bells, pass down streets that always seem deserted. The long sunless paragraphs, often going on for three pages or more, come to us in an English so antique that it seems a foreign tongue: words like "contagion" and "perdition" recur, we are introduced to "boatmen" and "watchmen." Our first impression may be of Nabokov lost inside a haunted house.

Yet part of what possesses one about these passages is that Sebald gives us nothing to hold on to, no background or cause and effect: nothing except the seraphic scraps that seem to belong to the album of a person now departed. His journeys are never undertaken in a spirit of adventure or delight—they often take place in areas or on trains that have unexplained "unpleasant associations" for him—and they never come to any discernible end. Often, unsettlingly, they pass between this world and the next, dreams and a kind of waking. As he wanders around Italy in the second section of *Vertigo,* the narrator spots Dante, then King Ludwig II of Bavaria; more often, though, he looks at the people around him and sees "a circle of severed heads" or (in Venice, of all places) "a moving cortege." Everything comes to him from very far away, with some dimension missing: people are seen moving in slow motion and there is a soundlessness, a stillness, to everything, as if it were being seen through several panes of glass. The narrator himself hardly knows whether he is in the "land of the living or already in another place."

Sebald has only to open an old book, in fact, to see, inside the front cover, the name of a person no longer alive. The only attachment he confesses to in the three works is one Clara, but both times she appears, it is in the context of a death. An innkeeper has only to touch him, indeed, and the narrator starts, with a sense of something "ghoulish or disembodied." Though it's customary to refer to a writer of such impeccable prose as writing like an angel, in the case of Sebald, sitting alone on a bench at twilight and presenting us with nothing but his back, it might be truer to say that he writes like a wraith.

And the theme of all his books is, at some level, nothing more than the effects they pass on to us: of restlessness, of panic, of being caught up in a lightless labyrinth (the shadow of Kafka is everywhere in these stories). The titles themselves announce their subjects as vertigo, the fact of being saturnine (*The Rings of Saturn*), and a compulsion to wander (*The Emigrants*). In some ways Sebald is working, with his hypnotic, spellbound prose, to put us into the very state he inhabits, unmoored, at a loss, in the dark. Lacking all explanations, offering no sense of before and after, his journeys come to us a little as the Ancient Mariner's come to Coleridge's wedding guest.

The only things that do fit together here, moreover, are coincidences, which impart a sense of being caught up in some script written by Fates we can't imagine to be benign (a believer, in most religions, holds that nothing is an accident—all is mandated by God; Sebald gives us the shadow side of that condition). Thus at one point the narrator leads a madman to the St. Agnes home, and we notice from the date given a little later that it is close to Saint Agnes' Eve. He tells us the story of Casanova, and we recall, a little unsettlingly, that Stendhal, in the first movement of the book, died on the street now known as rue Danielle-Casanova. The archetypal Sebald moment, you could say, comes when he walks into a pizza parlor in Verona (a pizza parlor!), and sees that the owner's name is Carlo Cadavero (lest this detail seem too Sebaldian to be true, he offers us a photograph of his bill from the restaurant). Later, returning to the place, he finds it all boarded up, blinds drawn on the apartment above, and the photographer next door so silent that we can only assume that the poor Cadavero has attained the state of his name. The odd keepsakes pasted into the text—here we see a picture of the shuttered restaurant—have the almost desperate air of pieces of evidence in a trial, aimed to show us (or the narrator himself) that all this really happened and he is not, in fact, mad.

Just as I was writing this sentence, I should here note, my partner came into the room, looking pale, and told me that, on a routine trip to the office just now, she had come upon a dead body laid out on the station platform. A long white sheet, she said, and a woman's shoes protruding from under it. I went into the next room—this is in Japan—to the desk I share with her teenage daughter, and saw on it a sample English-language sentence: "Last night there was a fire in our neighborhood, and an old woman burned to death." Clearly, the spell was working.

Sebald is always scrupulous with dates and street names and places—as if, again, to try to convince himself and us that all he is recording is not just the product of a deranged imagination—and if you read *Vertigo* on the factual level, its first section is an account of the life of Stendhal, and his trials in love and war. He became fascinated, we are told, with a woman of "great melancholy beauty," and, soon thereafter, we are shown a picture of some hands (the woman's?), another photo, of a pair of eyes (Stendhal's?), then a drawing of an ulcer. The writer's one inescapable theme, we read, before his death from syphilis, was "What is it that undoes a writer?"

The second section of the book follows the Sebald-seeming narrator's journey through Vienna, Venice, and Verona in 1980, in search, he only suggests, of details about the life of Kafka and clues about a series of grisly cult murders. The third movement tells us the story of Dr. K., another man tortured in life and love (and at this point the sharp-eyed reader may notice that some of the images, the cadences, even the details and events of *Vertigo* come from Kafka's terrifying story of a dead man's tale, "The Hunter Graccus"). And in the closing section of the book, the narrator returns to his hometown in Germany, which he can only bear to call "W." (though the dust jacket matter-of-factly identifies it as Wertach im Allgäu).

Across the four narratives images recur and echo like footsteps in a labyrinth, and with each recurrence their air of portent or meaning (albeit a meaning we can't guess, or perhaps don't want to know) intensifies. We see, again and again, in different contexts, people waving as on a distant ship, as if about to voyage off (as Sebald might put it) to the other shore. We revert frequently to a man (now the narrator, now Dr. K.) lying in a small hotel room, arms crossed behind his head, as the sounds of life come to him from the street outside. We see glimpses of "dust-blown expanses and tidal plains" that are, we are told, the landscape of the future. The force of these recurrences—even a sign above the narrator, when arriving in Milan, says LA PROSSIMA COINCIDENZA—is to make us feel as if we're simply sleepwalking through some diabolical plot that we can't follow. More than once, the narrator notices, in Italy, two men, always walking together, watching him from afar; later we learn that two men, always walking together, have been arrested in connection with the ritual murders.

It doesn't matter whether these are the same two men; what is important is that the narrator thinks they are: irrational fear and a sense of being hunted are the only home Sebald knows. He is like someone who has fallen through a trapdoor into some parallel world in which correspondences and patterns impress themselves more forcibly than does the real stuff of life. Thus the action proceeds (in his mind) almost like an allegory (and those two men come to seem agents of Charon, waiting to carry the narrator away); certain obvious things have no meaning, and certain covert things have too much. At one point, in an inn, another visitor (German, of course) makes off, by mistake, with the narrator's passport, and we feel that his very identity has been stolen. He buys a map in Milan, to guide him through the city, and on the cover is a labyrinth.

The reader who declines to succumb to the spell will say that Sebald is seeking out—to some extent creating—a world that will mirror his own brokenheartedness and dread; it is nearly always twilight in his stories, and the season he keeps returning to is autumn (especially November, "the month of the dead," as he characteristically calls it). The year with which he is fascinated in *Vertigo* is 1913, a time when everything, to us now, seems shadowed by what came soon thereafter, making even the tiniest detail (an inscription in a book, dated 1913) seem haunted. To some extent Sebald is almost addicted to the dark, and when he makes for an "unprepossessing, ill-omened hotel" on arrival in Milan, it's no surprise that the "wizen-faced creature" who receives him there resembles all the other dwarves and misshapen beings we've met.

Sebald would reply that this is precisely his point: to one born with his legacy, all life is a *memento mori*. He is running from a world in his head from which there can be no release but death. And the figures on the far-off ship, so hushed from afar, give the impression they are heading to a place from which they will never return; the outline of a lone man, in a small dark room, begins to seem a metaphor for the narrator's life, alone in a temporary habitation, laid out as in his resting place, the sounds of real life coming to him at a distance. To a dead man, Sebald might be saying, all the world's a funeral.

Such grim and comfortless sensations would no doubt make for very painful reading were it not for the "great melancholy beauty" of the prose, which even in translation (by the poet Michael Hulse, but surely with more than a little help from the English-fluent Sebald) rises to a pitch of antique sonorousness and majesty that makes everything else one comes across seem small. The spirits hovering over it—or behind it—are Robert Burton, author of *The Anatomy of Melancholy*, and Sebald's fellow East Anglian, Sir Thomas Browne, who once wrote that if you watch sleeping bodies from on high, and pass across the globe, following the setting sun, you can imagine the whole world to be a city of the dead (the image is so dear to Sebald that he uses it twice). Though Sebald's flights are seldom flights in the modern aeronautic sense—he usually travels by foot, or on a boat or train—they do offer the prospect of the world as seen from a very great height (as in the light of Eternity, or death). Their psychological key might be said to be the word *"unheim-lich"*—or "uncanny"—a Freudian term that has to do with "obsessive paths of action," a "repetition compulsion," and what one scholar calls "a flood of repressed memories that fill the subject with both dread and pleasure." (Two years after writing this sentence, I might add, I found that one of Sebald's untranslated critical works was actually called *Unheimliche Heimat*, or "Unhomelike Home.")

The Emigrants introduced us in the English-speaking world to this new kind of travel writing, and as one proceeds through it—noting, very slowly, that its subject is all the things that are being forcibly left out or suppressed (the empty rooms and blank pages of the last days of the war)—one begins to see that the very title, so hopeful in another context, in this book has much more a sense of the fugitive (a sense that comes over more strongly in the German title of the work, *Die Ausgewanderten*). Its subject is really the people who are forced out of one world and yet never really arrive in another, and so pass all their days as specters of a kind, not really living and not truly dead.

Those who concluded from that book that Sebald was writing about the Holocaust had to revise their opinions with the translation of *The Rings of Saturn,* for that work suggests a much larger sense of desolation. As Sebald's narrator wanders around the lonely empty spaces of England—always the last passenger on the bus, the only guest at the inn—all he sees are ruined castles, abandoned factories, cemeteries that are overgrown. And the pressing sense on every side of the end of Empire pushes him towards much larger thoughts of ruin and decline (to a Buddhist, he might be reminding us, every meeting ends in a departure). The book begins with its narrator in a hospital "in a state of almost total immobility."

In *Vertigo,* the sense of exile becomes most apparent when the narrator returns to his hometown. His family home has been turned into a hotel, he finds, and, checking in, he can only identify himself as a "foreign correspondent" (even as, of course, living in East Anglia, he writes in a language that none of his neighbors can follow). Every afternoon he sits alone in the "empty bar room," and in the evenings he watches the regulars from the corner, a kind of shellshocked Rip Van Winkle. Those who find this too metaphorical to be true might here recall that the opening movement of the book told us that everything that Stendhal remembered of the campaign in Italy was a fiction: what is important is not just what happened, but what our fevered minds imagine to have happened.

At one point, though—and just in time, perhaps—as he sits on a Tyrolean bus full of old crones complaining about the darkness and the rain, their blighted crops, suddenly the sun comes out and floods the green pastures with a kind of radiance (and, it must be said, angels are one of the presences that recur in *Vertigo*). Even the Italian titles he gives to two sections of his book seem, now, to be ways to try to alchemize his dark memories into something else, in a more sunlit, hopeful tongue; part of his lifelong flight from German. His theme, after all, is not the people destroyed by the war, but those only wounded, permanently incapacitated by it, the sound of knelling bells always in the distance.

Those who hear that Sebald's books are part of a never-ending excavation of memory may wonder about his relation to the poet of the cork-lined room, likewise famous for his short-ness of breath. Yet where memory in Proust seems to bring back lost loves and careless afternoons, in Sebald it can only conjure up the dead. The memories that await him in his hometown are all of hearses and sudden deaths; of unexplained departures, or people who live their lives mute and stunned in their own rooms. (The fact, only slipped in, that the narrator's father served in the Reich becomes the least terrifying detail of all.)

A closer parallel is with that other maker of obsessive jour-neys, Melville, afflicted as he was with a sense of being caught in a tangle of the Fates, and yet committed to exploring deeps that were inseparable from the dark. Think of how Ishmael, a proto-Sebald, talks in the opening paragraph of *Moby-Dick* of how he goes off to sea whenever he feels "a damp drizzly November in my soul" and notices himself passing coffin warehouses. And yet the intensity, even the delirium, of Melville comes from our sense that his craziness is carrying him away, as strong waves might the sturdiest boat. What terrifies in Sebald is, if anything, the opposite: his almost posthumous calm, as of a frozen ship upon a frozen ocean.

"Nature is a Haunted House," he might be saying, with Emily Dickinson, "Art—a House that tries to be haunted."

2000

A
NEW
YEAR

On the minivan, driving through the deserted moon-scape of the East, not far from Djibouti—it could be not far from almost anywhere—I found myself next to a man, a former journalist, who exulted in the chance to talk about his trip to London, and asked me how Broadway was doing (compared, he said, with those other centers of world culture, Frankfurt Airport and Heathrow). The man on the other side of me, an agricultural student, looked on with wonder at these signs of worldliness. It was coming on for New Year, and a new page in Ethiopian history. The country had held its first free elections in sixteen hundred years, and everyone now was waiting to see how the three-year-old government of Meles Zenawi would fare. After centuries of emperors, and seventeen years of Communist madness at the hands of Colonel Mengistu, Ethiopia was trying the new Western tool of democracy.

"All politics is prostitution," the man (whose family name was Flahflah) pronounced, and the agricultural student nodded meaningfully. "Rome was not built in a day." He talked of how the English had devastated India, how despots were as much a part of his history as of Europe's, how all men were brothers.

"Americans say democracy, English say democracy," he went on. "But this imported democracy is sometimes inapplicable. Look at me: I am a Moslem, I have four wives, seven children. In my home, I must make all the decisions. I do not allow the debate. I am in control. So how can I talk about democracy in the country when I do not allow it at home?"

He pulled up his monogrammed briefcase, and showed me a diploma from Egypt, from fourteen years before. He had dined with many famous men, he said. "We in Africa are very low. So our leaders are very low. But in Washington, a man from the international aid development office, a very high man, I talked to him, he took me to lunch, and he said, 'Here in America also, it is corrupt. But here, the difference is, a man chooses his friends, and they are qualified. In Africa, a leader chooses his friends, and they are illiterate—and he does not choose the qualified man.' But it is the same. Tribalism in both cases, but we call it something different."

Zenawi was not perfect, he acknowledged, but nor was Bill Clinton. "What you say in office, and what you say out of office, they are never the same. Too many interests."

The agricultural student nodded once more.

Back in Addis Ababa, the rich Indians were taking drinks on the veranda of Unity House, while local trendies revved up their

Toyotas (with Harvard University stickers on them) and pale expats sweetened up their local girlfriends. Addis is almost like a rough draft of a capital, or an *esprit d'escalier*—a clever idea that came too late—with its buildings (OFFICE OF THE AD HOC COMMITTEE FOR PEACE AND DEVELOPMENT) set against outstretched beggars, and its signs (ADDIS ABABA SHERATON PROJECT) pointing to vacant lots. It is also, like many capitals in politically unstable countries (like Cairo, or Delhi, or Manila, say), a city of whispers. At the next table in the Beijing Restaurant, two Africans were thrashing out "Realpolitik" and "alternative programs," while, outside, the Mercedes of the hotels and the purring BMWs of the Amhara elite carried their passengers to Christmas feasts, or to places like the Ghion Riviera, where a black-tie band was serenading the plump, and girls were crooning love songs in front of the sunlit swimming pool ("It is strictly forbidden to swim immediately after taking meals").

"They are brutalizing the country," said one of the men in the next booth, feelingly. "It is a revolution ten times more powerful than Mengistu's revolution. Because that was based on—nothing. This is based on people's deepest feelings."

"Yah, man. It is like the prisoners in the Greek myth, who for thirty years took the shade as reality. They took the shade for reality!"

They talked about the BBC World Service, while outside the former officers of Mengistu's army walked the streets, trying to hit up foreigners for money, and children banged on cars at stoplights, crying, "Father, father! By Jesus Christ! Hungry people!"

The next day, a society matron slipped her jeep down Churchill Road, past the Kid's Paradise school, towards a jeweler she knew. "For me, they are heroes, the guerrilla leaders," she said, taking time off from her own jewelry business, and collecting her sons from school in Switzerland. "But they are kids. Sometimes they come to my house and say, 'We do not have any more than a fifth-grade education. And now it is too late to go to school.' And I tell them, 'Why do you worry about education? You have been giving your lives to your country. That is more important.'"

That evening, a large man at the wheel of his small car, with a cauliflower ear, said, "Zenawi will kill democracy. But still, this is not Africa. I talk to the foreigners, and they tell me in Lagos, in Algiers, it is never safe. Ethiopia is not like that." A little later he added, "I tried to go to the U.S. But the Embassy, they tell me no. Is too much of our people going to U.S. Now they say, no more."

The notices outside the Hilton hotel—the only spot of glamour in the country—said, "The Hotel is not liable for any damage or threat occurring to or from vehicles parked in this courtyard." The papers in the lobby were ten days old. In the coffee shop they were playing Muzaked versions of Christmas songs, culminating in "Do They Know It's Christmas?"—the song recorded to provide food for the starving of Ethiopia.

The banners across the street said STREETCHILDREN WEEK, and the books in the window of the Ethiopian Book Centre were *World Blindness and Its Prevention*, *Brain's Diseases of the Nervous System*, and *America: Life and Institutions*. Boys sold candies (individually) on street corners, or put out scales so that people could weigh themselves (for a price). In the National Stadium, a soccer team with red shorts and white shirts was playing against a team with red shirts and white shorts.

In my own hotel, the Ghion, an infamous Somali warlord was staying in the Riviera wing (taking note, no doubt, of the stern rules outside the swimming pool: "If you feel tired while swimming, inform immediately"). I stood on the lawn outside his room, under a huge full moon, while his fluent and charis-matic private secretary, until recently an M.B.A. student, told me that they were trying only to get "democracy and justice for our country," a "Somalia ruled by Somalis." They had come here to broker peace. "When the Americans came," the young man went on, "we greeted them with green leaves, green flowers. But now the Western propaganda has distorted all that. We are not afraid to die."

I turned to my local guidebook. "The first thing that strikes you about Addis Ababa," it informed me, as guidebooks do, "is the champagne atmosphere."

1993

FLIGHTS

The great courage is still
to gaze as squarely at the
light as at death.

—CAMUS

THE

KHAREEF

When the southwestern monsoon, or *khareef*, passes through the southern tip of Arabia, a heavy chill mist falls over the province of Dhofar, in southern Oman, and the temperatures fall twenty or thirty degrees below those of the rest of the Arabian peninsula. In the thick fog you can hear almost nothing but the ocean sighing in the distance, and when you travel up into the mountains it's hard to see anything but women veiled in black from head to toe, only their mascara'ed eyes looking out, and locals seated on patches of green beside the road, delightedly picnicking in the rain.

The *khareef* is an eerie, somewhat magical time in southern Oman, and its heavy fogs and rain allow the frankincense trees to grow along the foothills that run beside the sea. Drizzle is imminent nearly always, and the mist envelops everything, so that when you look down the long empty roads you see camels, and sand, and nothingness. Along one side of the road sits a Hilton hotel, but the palm trees beside it are worn, and the gusty ocean is almost entirely without color. The world has sloughed off proportion and dimension.

The smell of frankincense on the back streets, the Indian shopkeepers outside their little stalls as if they were still in Cochin—"Foodstuff and Luxuries," "Watch Repair," "Coconut Sale," "Auto Cushion"—suggest somewhere entirely forgotten by the world. Everything shuts down in the middle of the day, though not for prayer; the sovereign spirits here are trade and sleep. Once the richest area in the world, Dhofar now nestles behind the mountains, unvisited, much like the last sultan, who took to his palace here for twelve years, and banned bicycles, radios, even sunglasses for locals.

I sat in my room in the deserted hotel sometimes, and watched a few American soldiers, on their Friday off, wrestle on the lawn below. The sound of Arabic curses came from the next terrace; in the lobby there were always barrel-chested Englishmen, here to train the local army, with tattoos across their forearms, pounding one fist into another, again and again and again.

The Indians sat at their desks looking wistful, sometimes wry. What had brought them here, I asked. Not adventure or dreams or anything; a shrug, an uncle now gone. They'd come to Muscat, the fairy-tale sand-city in the north, and somehow ended up here. What was there to do? A defeated smile.

In the bar, a tiny Filipina served drinks to tired blond Germans with leathery tans, who shook their bangles and tossed their heads impatiently, as they waited for the grand tours they'd been promised, and groups of men from Atlanta in shorts—who knew on what mission?—cracked jokes as they sat in the thick armchairs huddled together in clusters in the lobby. "The plural of 'fish' is 'fishes'?" "A dollar for anyone in the room who can tell us what the plural of 'fish' is."

The Omanis in their long white robes sat in the vast space talking softly, their women dressed in black, so intense that they seemed apparitions of suggestiveness. A curling hand, decorated with some kind of design; a kohl-lined eye. So little could be seen of them, walking straight and regal in their black, handbags swinging from their shoulders, white clogs emerging occasionally under their robes, that their eyes carried everything. A spark, a light of mischief.

Outside my window there was dust and fog; out on the road, spotless tarmac stretching in every direction without cease. Camels by the sand, and in the distance the new port, to receive container ships. The mountains were close, but nothing but clouds now; figures appeared around curves like creatures from myth, and then disappeared again into the mist.

I arrived here after a thirty-three-hour flight from Santa Barbara to Los Angeles to London, then Abu Dhabi, to Muscat, and then Salalah; I got out at the long dusty road and walked into a room with a terrace, a view of the sea without color. In the morning, when I went out, there was rain all over the chairs; a lone figure was somewhere behind the palm trees, walking towards the lights.

One day I hired a car and driver—a homesick man from Kerala, on his way to marry a woman he'd never met (he kept up with home at night through his FM radio)—and we drove into the hills. As we went up the mountains from the plain, the mist, already thick, began to envelop us, so we were part of it, and it of us, and the rain began to fall. Cars inched their way around turns, and at the tomb of Job, at the top, I stepped out into the lightly falling rain and followed a group of shadows, all in black, disappearing between the trees.

We drove down again, and south, and found ourselves in a paradise of sorts, a clear river running along the base of the hills, where happy shirtless boys were splashing and jumping around as if they'd found their way back to the beginning of the world. Families were gathered on carpets under the trees, one man serenading his party—a wedding party—with a set of bagpipes.

Near the Holiday Inn, a crumbling ruin not far away, archaeologists had found the remains of the place acclaimed by Marco Polo as a "fine and great and noble city." The Queen of Sheba had sent her dhows from here, my guide said, to Egypt and Jerusalem and Rome, bearing frankincense at a time when it was worth more than gold. Her castle was now remembered by a pile of stones.

In the lobby a Canadian engineer sat alone, looking out into the mist where the GIs organized games of touch football without a ball.

Four days later, following the so-called Incense Coast, I came to Aden, the largest port of southern Yemen, which once had seemed a center of the world, the place where every ship from Britain to India stopped for refueling. The last time I had been here, at the age of two, in 1959—my mother was taking me back from the Oxford where I was born to the Bombay that was her hometown—Aden had buzzed with the slightly illicit excitement that attends a port, groups of touts out to meet the tourist ships and promise everything that is possible when West first touches East. Aden, Victoria's first imperial acquisition, was the largest harbor in the world then, outside Manhattan.

Now, in the summer of 2001, the town was a biblical wasteland. Goats foraged outside the broken shops and old women, at
occasional red lights, came and hammered on the windows of
passing cars, skinny arms extended. I saw no shops or restaurants
or anythings in Aden; the children played in the street because
there was nowhere else for them to play. It seemed as if the whole
city was sitting on debris, waiting to see what the next wind
would blow into town.

I took myself to the Crescent Hotel, near Steamer Point,
where a replica of Big Ben tolled the passing hours. But when I
walked into the old British haunt—a black-and-white portrait
of Queen Elizabeth, when young, peering out through the unlit
lobby—I quickly realized this was no place to stay. "We have a
new Crescent Hotel down the street," the young boy at the desk
offered, and I followed him to a marginally less dusty place
where an aged retainer offered me a crisp military salute.

The new hotel on the beach seemed more promising, though
just to walk into the lobby I had to walk through a security
machine of the kind you see at airports. Going out onto the
sand—pristine, and opening onto a silent, lovely bay—I noticed
that I was the only person there. Then I looked more closely and
saw armed soldiers on both sides of me, standing against the
wall, protecting me, I could only imagine, from Aden.

When I walked out of the hotel, a sad-eyed man, apparently
Indian, slouched up to me. He said hello in a fluent, almost swallowed English, and I learned that his father had been an Englishman, though born here. The man before me had applied for
a passport, and the chance to live in England, but Her Majesty's
Government had refused him because his father, though entirely
English, was born in Aden. "Do you want to see the cemetery?"
he said.

We drove a few hundred yards to where a clump of head-stones sat in the wasting heat. Their inscriptions were in German, Greek, Russian, or Chinese; Aden had once been known as the "entrance-hall of China and the warehouse of the West." Most of the inscriptions, though, were in English, recalling forgotten Gwendolenes and Despinas, flying officers and telegraphists. OH FOR A TOUCH OF THAT VANISHED HAND. AVE ATQUE VALE.

"We used to see them every time we went to church," my new friend said. "Getting buried. One or two a week." Now St. Mary's was shuttered, and Christians such as he could worship only in secret if at all. The English had left, quite literally overnight, in 1967, the Russians had come in, and then they too had given up on Aden, leaving it to a civil war. Though technically reunited with the northern parts of the country in 1991, it had been through a two-month siege in 1994. The Frontier Hotel, burned out, had become the Mövenpick. The Mövenpick, destroyed in the next period of fighting, was now the Aden Hotel.

In the small part of town where the English had been, the signs still said, WE HOPE YOU ENJOYED YOUR STAY. PLEASE COME AGAIN at the Prince of Wales pier. A bookshop in the customs shed sold black-and-white postcards of the once bustling port, and paperbacks, forty years old, in which someone had laboriously inscribed, *Miss Sirihin Abdullah Murji, P.O. Box* 1959, *Mombasa.* I thought of a grandfather, difficult and vainglorious in his youth, who now has been softened by incapacity, and can almost be regarded with affection.

We drove around to see the small museum and the Rambow Tourist Restaurant and Cafeteria, where Rimbaud once had lived. And when I walked into the hotel, that evening, the man who had offered to reconfirm my ticket, to Jeddah next day, came up with a smile. "Your flight is canceled," he said (and having seen Aden, I was surprised they even made the pretense of flights). "But there's another one in four days' time."

Four days, I thought, could be forty in this wilderness, so I went outside, found an old African man with a battered car, and we drove into the deserted downtown area known as Crater. In the Yemenia office a woman in a black veil looked out at me, preparing for hostilities, and then turned away to a friend.

"It's important that I get to Jeddah tomorrow. I'll take any flight that's available."

"One moment," she said, and then turned to the little girl who had appeared by her desk and joked about their friends, a birthday party coming up, perhaps. Then, turning to the computer, she slowly tapped on a few keys and then, looking at her watch, said, "There's a flight to the capital, but it leaves ten minutes from now."

"I have to be out of Aden," I said. "There must be something leaving." She stirred, and yawned, and went over to talk to another friend. There seemed no point in hurrying; no one was going anywhere in Aden.

Then, coming back and tapping away at her computer again, she said, "There is a flight leaving in the morning. But from Sana'a, across the mountains. A six-hour drive away." It left at 6:00 a.m., which meant that check-in was seven hours from now.

"I'll take it."

"I can't help you with this. You must go to the other Yemenia office."

I went out into the dark—the main street was like the cemetery—and roused the driver from his sleep; we rattled off to another Yemenia office, a few hundred yards away, where another woman in a black veil looked up at me.

This new adversary clicked away on her keyboard—computers are slow in Aden, and linked to a world no one really believes in—and then, after many blocked paths and wrong turns, she announced that a plane was leaving in the morning, from Sana'a, the capital, long enemy territory to Aden, six hours away across the mountains. Check-in was six hours from now, she said; I couldn't make it.

Time slips away in a place like Aden; space itself dissolves, as if the whole city is drifting away on the narcotic *qat* that everyone chews. The clock at the top of the Crescent Hotel clearly hadn't moved for years.

I bought a ticket from her—no price was too high—and went out to summon my driver again, to drive back to the hotel. I called the hotel in advance, from the Yemenia office, to fix up a taxi to drive to the capital, and we made our way back, at a donkey's pace, through the broken center of the city, past roadblocks and detours, the large ditches Chinese laborers were digging on behalf of the Aden Sewage Company. The city is stretched out along the coast like a piece of gum that someone has been chewing for a very long time.

At the hotel, racing to collect my things and check out, I was told that the taxi had been called for, but showed no signs of arriving; it was better to go to the taxi stand at the bus station. A young employee in a suit pushed me into a minivan, and we drove, tires squealing, across town, skidding in the dust, to a bus station that was a dingy emptiness. In front of what was optimistically called the "taxi stand" there was darkness and silence.

At last a man appeared, smiling, in an old Peugeot, and I recognized a man who had taken me all around town two days before in search of a cemetery we never found. "Wait over there," he said, pointing to an even darker corner of the empty lot, and we went and sat in the silence, the night. The young man in his suit drummed his fingers on the dashboard; he looked at his watch, looked back nervously at me. Finally, the man who had cheated me before appeared, at the wheel of a very old car.

He had no interest in driving himself, he explained, through the man in the suit—the main source of income in the mountains was the kidnapping of foreigners. But he had found someone else who knew so little, or needed so much, that he had volunteered for the job: a very old man in a dirty turban loomed out of the dark. As he took his place behind the wheel, eyes closed, and visibly shaking, friends came up and patted him on the back, wished him luck, said prayers for his safe return.

He, too, before moving, closed his eyes and muttered a quick prayer, and then we were off, in the dark, the old man hardly able to see over the wheel, peering out into the night. Occasional trucks came barreling towards us on the narrow road, their headlights blinding.

The night that followed never happened, I tell myself now; it belongs to some place in the imagination. Very soon we were on a mountain road, pitch black, and though I could see nothing around us, I could tell there was a sheer drop on one side. Above us, as we climbed, there were occasional towers, medieval fortresses, set across the hillside. We turned a mountain corner, and suddenly there was noise: men with guns, turbaned boys, a clamor of faces in the dark motioning for us to stop. A flashlight in my eyes, my passport taken away, a whispered confabulation. The driver, trembling, was asked to get out and open up the back.

Then, as suddenly as they had materialized, the guns were gone again, and we were bumping along in the dark, mountains on one side of us, a precipice on the other. I tried to sleep, but every time I fell away—seven, ten times in the night—I woke to find us stopped, guns in front of us, and faces at the window. The driver shoving banknotes into a hand, or laboring out to what looked like a rebel guardpost. Boys, clamorous, full of their own strength, asking who I was, peering in to get a look.

There were painted windows made of glass in the six- or seven-story houses beside us and when the lights were on, the panes shone like stained-glass across the darkened mountainside. Sometimes, as I slept, I woke to rain, the creaking wipers of the car moving frantically back and forth while the car skidded across the road and the man swerved furiously, so we were spinning towards the mountain. At times he turned on a radio—mad wailing in the dark—to keep himself from falling asleep, his stash of *qat* beside him.

When there was a light above us on the road, I looked at my watch—11:41, 1:53. The capital never seemed to come closer. The driver stopped, to relieve himself in a ditch. Again, to get some warmer clothing out of the back. He stopped again, to catch his breath, and I pointed angrily at my watch; he came back from his stop with a can of 7-Up, two bars of chocolate, for me.

Occasionally, we passed a sudden light in the dark mountains—a circle of figures around a shack for some reason open at 2 a.m. Then, it was only darkness again, the plain far below, the sound of thunder from the mountains. Rain, and boys waving at us to stop; guns at the window, and the air appreciably cooler in the high places, the tower-houses all around shuttered fastnesses.

As the first call to prayer rose up—3:45, I guessed—we came to what seemed to be buildings, larger roads (the capital?), and boys who now stood at intersections in the brownish light. Guarding their turf as if in East L.A., oil drums blocking the way, and coming to our window to demand tithes, local taxes, or blood money. The driver turned left onto an empty road, then right onto an empty road, and I realized that he had no idea where he was going.

At last, long after 4:00 a.m., we saw a tower, even higher than the tower-houses all around, and I recognized the building where I had been admitted into the country a few days before, the *khareef* just behind me. A group of Chinese traders was passing through a security check; a man who slept on the sofa in his office got up to offer me Saudi rials. I got in a plane and flew to Dubai—Internet connections in the airport hotel, a seven-star hotel only a short drive away—and saw the monitors at every departure gate announcing New York, London, Tokyo.

Less than six weeks later, as it happened, two planes flew into the World Trade Center in New York, and Aden, Oman, were suddenly pulled out of the subconscious, back into the forefront of our minds. The bored soldiers I had seen in the hotel lobby began steaming towards Afghanistan, to fight, and southern Yemen, near Aden, where Osama bin Laden was born, was taken to be the center of all evil. Aden, everyone now recalled, was the site of the most recent terrorist attack on America (the bombing of the USS *Cole* eleven months before, in the harbor outside my hotel), and a place that most of us had consigned to myth, somewhere behind the mists of the *khareef,* was suddenly dragged back into the present tense.

I sat in California and listened to the imprecations—Aden now deemed the opposite of Milton's "Araby the Blest"—and thought back to the driver who had got out in the middle of the night to buy me chocolate, the woman turning to the little girl in the airline office, my sad-eyed guide pointing to the graves of his mother, his sister, the Indian nuns, the British officers. Many of them, I suspected, had friends and loved ones of their own in New York (even in the World Trade Center), whom they must be worried about even now. In the streets—it wasn't hard to imagine—the children would be playing tag in the dusk, their high voices rising up along the empty boulevards, while we sat in our mansions, watching versions of their lives onscreen, and wishing destruction on them all.

2001

A
JOURNEY
INTO
LIGHT

If you look at Bolivia in a certain light—and light is the sovereign element here, glinting off the tin roofs of the valley and turning the windows of the high-rises into panes of gold—the city of La Paz offers a visitor a near-perfect diagram of the tenses. Right at the center of town is a model of the colonial past: a classic Spanish plaza with a legislative palace on one side of it, a presidential palace (and a cathedral) on another, and, on a third, the "Gran Hotel Paris," a now-fading relic of yesterday's glories that beams out the single word "Paris" across the skyline after dark. At the center of the plaza is a statue—GLORY, UNION, PEACE, and FORCE, cry out its four sides—and all around it are nymphs, standing for some of the classical arts.

Just a few minutes' walk away from that official center of imported power is what might seem to be the present tense: the flower-filled elegance of the Prado, the closest thing La Paz offers to a grand avenue in New York. Indian women are everywhere on the sidewalk, occupying every nook and cranny of free space with their pyramids of Pringles cans, their pirated videos of Ricky Martin, and enough copies of Peter Drucker's works on neoliberalism to occupy the citizenry for a century. But all these sights are dwarfed by the signs of modernity all around. Outside a chic McDonald's an armed man stands guard, protecting a place whose prices are higher than those of the Parisian café next door. Across the street are kids with cell phones, and Internet cafés. At the place where the boulevard ends, a long straggly line of laborers is gathered, almost every day, around the base of a plate-glass skyscraper on which, too fittingly, is written, THE FUTURE OF BOLIVIA.

In fact that future lies a few minutes' drive away, through Sopapachi (the embassy area, full of "Latin jazz" clubs and Tex-Mex hangouts), down in the valley to the south. The Burger King in the Zona Sur is as large as a Mercedes showroom, and the Hypermarket on the corner seems to invert everything that swarms and sprawls across the Indian market up above. The names that govern the straight streets are the traditional ones— "Calacoto" and "Cotacota," "Achumani" and "Chasquipampa"— and yet the whole clean suburb has been made to look like what the affluent, at least, might hope for in the future. The karaoke parlor here is called "America," and the shopping mall "San Diego." As I sat one night in a pizza joint, which boasted prices higher than in Miami, a high-school girl at the next table, soignée as Catherine Zeta-Jones, shut her eyes and sang along, transported, to "Hotel California" on the sound track.

Yet the saving grace of Bolivia, and what makes it almost irresistible for anyone eager to escape the simplicities of the moment, is that in reality it stands all such theories on their heads. The actual center of town, just blocks away from the Spanish Plaza Murillo, is the Indian marketplace, the living past, where women in bowler hats offer llama foetuses and aphrodisiacs along with copies of Francis Fukuyama's *The End of History*. The costumes they are wearing are themselves something of an illusion: the plaits, many-colored ponchos, and bowler hats that we take to be such a picturesque aspect of the native culture, are, in fact, the result of the mandate of an eighteenth-century Spanish king. And where in cities like Lima you may occasionally see a splash of Indian culture in the middle of what is really a Spanish city, in La Paz it can be startling to see occasional pieces of Spain in what is, to all intents and purposes, a province of the fourteenth century. The future, you cannot help but feel, lies for Bolivia in its past.

The traveler, if he comes from a place of comfort, travels, in part, to be stood on his head; to lose track of tenses, or at least to be back to essentials, free of the details of home. "Teach me," as Thomas Merton wrote in his journal, "to go to a country without names and words and terms." Yet if he is to travel far enough away from the places he knows, the traveler is also obliged to see everything in two ways, or two languages, at once. On the one hand, he's a newcomer who's walking down the street, unable to read the signs, with the map in his hand held upside down; on the other, he has traveled to look at himself (and his world) through the eyes of the local, for whom the real source of comedy and strangeness is that newcomer, walking the wrong way down the street.

In Bolivia, this doubleness confounds you at every turn, in the most indigenous country in South America, where the people around you are speaking a language for which there is not even any written form. And so all the guidebook facts, the World Bank figures, that you've brought along with you go swiftly out the window. You've read, perhaps, in the *New York Times* that Bolivia suffers from the worst rural poverty in the world (97 percent of the people in the countryside, according to the U.N., live below the poverty level); yet as you walk along the Prado, fathers bouncing their children on their shoulders while Goofy and Mickey share a sleigh with three rival Santas, "poverty" is not the first word that comes to mind. You've seen, no doubt, in the *Guinness Book of World Records* that Bolivia enjoys the unhappy distinction of having suffered more changes in government than any other country (188 in 157 years); yet as you stroll among its people, girls drifting arm in arm with other girls, policemen walking hand in hand with their wives, a Nativity scene even above the Ministry of Justice, you can easily feel as if Bolivia has come to a kind of peace with its perpetual unrest; the word you hear most often is *tranquilo.* And you've read, if you've been to your local library, about a country filtered for us through accounts of Hunter Thompson and Che Guevara and Klaus Barbie (the ex-Nazi who lived in comfort in La Paz in the middle of the 1980s); yet when you arrive in La Paz, the light so resplendent that you feel as if you're very close to the heavens, the lovers pressing against one another in the shadows of the colonial quarter after dark, you wonder how much any foreign visitor can explain about the place.

Bolivia, in fact, stands apart from all your theories and ideas, much as the Indian women, with their boxes of Windows 98 software and books by the Dalai Lama, sit apart from the future that saunters past them on the street. As I walked through the city my first day in La Paz, the women who lined the sidewalks in their colorful clothing never once made an approach to me, or shouted anything out, or tried to catch my attention with their wares. They seemed content to sit where they were, as (it was easy to believe) they had always sat. When, once, the sky suddenly turned black and torrential rains began to pelt down on us all, they got up wordlessly, draped some tarpaulin over their shacks and then sat down again, as silent as before.

The other dimension that turns everything into uncertainty in La Paz is, of course, those very skies, which govern every moment and make the humans who walk under them seem very small indeed. Water boils at eighty degrees centigrade in the thin, unnatural air, and drivers have to let out the air from their tires before entering the city. Planes flying into La Paz have landing speeds less than half those they'd have in Lima (and when my own arrived, in a near-silent international terminal, all I saw was a Narcotics Control passport desk, unmanned; eleven little suitcases unloaded from my plane onto a solitary baggage carousel; and a small space marked out as an "Oxygen Room"). The friendly taxi driver who greeted me outside, with the warm, weathered face of Tibet, drove me through the shantytown of El Alto and into the great valley of light, and I realized, almost instantly, that I would have to learn to move and breathe differently in this city two miles above the sea.

I had strange dreams in La Paz every night, and awoke at three in the morning, convinced that I knew everything that was wrong with my life and my work (I would scribble down excited notes in the heat of inspiration, and, a little later, looking back on them, see nothing but hallucination). Often I would vomit on an empty stomach in those early days, or throw myself onto my bed in a fit of sleeplessness. A knock would come at my door, and I would stagger over to see a chamberman—Bolivia has men who clean hotel rooms, instead of women—standing silently in front of me with a tray of marzipans shaped to look like watermelon slices. Another knock would come and I would find a man at my door with a canister of oxygen for me to breathe.

I learned very soon, amidst Bolivia's turbulent skies—the sun picking out a single building in the far-off mountains, and the clouds lined with gold—that it was folly to plan anything; you are ruled by the heavens in La Paz. One bright afternoon, when the sun was so sharp above the snowcaps that they looked like painted ornaments—clouds in a different part of the city were weeping rain—I went out into the midsummer streets to go and visit the rock formations that sit beside the affluent houses of the Zona Sur. As I stepped into a minivan, a few drops of rain began to speckle the windshield.

Within ten minutes or so, following the mountain road that cuts through the city on one side, we were in the privileged world of condos and fancy new lodges. As we began to drive through the well-paved streets, suddenly the rain began to come down, and then hail, so furiously that we had to stop the car. We sat in the middle of the road and, all around, what looked to be a flurry of snow blanketed the whole city (so thick was the hail, so fierce). Brown waterfalls sprang to life in the slope around us, and the road that had brought us down into the valley was now a mountain path, impassable and icy. A few weeks later, a similar storm, depositing almost a gallon of water per square foot across the city in less than an hour, left boulevards and whole neighborhoods collapsed and took sixty-nine lives or more, the broad avenues of downtown turned, within minutes, into surging torrents, and the people who ran into underpasses to take shelter swept away along with everything else.

When at last the rain subsided and we labored our way back up into the center—the well-ordered streets looking now like a jungle—I asked a *paceño* in the car where the sacred sites of the city were, the places where the local people worshiped.

"Over there," he said, pointing to a hill on top of which there were no trees. "Wherever there is a space open to the skies."

Everywhere I looked, in short.

I had come to La Paz at the end of 2001 to get away from a world that was preoccupied with the war between the future and the past. A few weeks earlier the war had grown intense, as Islamic terrorists had sent two planes crashing into the World Trade Center in Manhattan, and the very symbol of the modern global order had gone down in flames. A few days later, in response, Washington, flailing around for something on which to take out its anger, had settled upon the past—an undeveloped Afghanistan ruled by a government that wanted to drag it back into an old world of veils and universal proscriptions. The Moslems, clothing themselves in the words of the Prophet, were calling, it seemed, for a return to the old ways, and to ancient notions of community and ritual and devotion; the postmodern order, by contrast, America—home of the very images that classic Islam forbids—was calling for a race into the future, the man-made, the new.

La Paz, however, seemed to sit outside all such ideas, and not only because it had few radical Moslems in residence, and not much investment in the future. For centuries the particular allure of the city named for peace had been that it sat apart from the world, off in its own dimension. Queen Victoria, in fact, had pronounced that Bolivia did not exist (when an ambassador of hers in La Paz refused a drink offered him by one of the country's tyrants, and was forced, in response, to drink a barrelful of coffee and be led backwards through the streets on a mule); Sir Arthur Conan Doyle, detective-story writer turned spiritualist, had set his "lost world" in Bolivia. During the 1980s, when all the world watched Washington and Moscow pronouncing "mutually assured destruction" on one another, La Paz was said to be the safest place to hide in the event of a nuclear crisis.

And even in the midst of all their very real problems—125 beds, so they said, to serve the fifty thousand physically and emotionally disturbed people in the slum of El Alto—the residents of La Paz seemed to have a very different notion of a "market economy" from the one unveiled by the young, Texas-educated local president of the time, speaking his fluent English on TV. In the week before I arrived in Bolivia, Argentina next door had seen three different presidents, and dozens of demonstrators lay dead along its elegant streets; on the way up to La Paz, I had stopped off in Lima, and found an angry, swollen metropolis across which people had scrawled cries of rage, and where even the windows were barred. Like many of the countries of South America, both Peru and Argentina seemed to have been left by the Spanish stuck between a vanished colonial notion of glory and a future that never arrived; in desperation, often, not fully European and not really themselves, they'd tried to make up the gap with pomp. Bolivia, by comparison, gave an impression of self-containment: a poor country, yes, but one that did not look as if it ever expected to be rich.

For me, then, Bolivia was pure magic. I drew back the curtains in my room and saw everything picked out with uncanny sharpness in the summer light. Mountains almost four miles high stood at the end of narrow streets, and at night the whole center of town began to glow with the lights of the little houses around the hills. The shantytown of El Alto, which I visited one morning, was a shocking place, in some ways, with its corrugated-iron shacks and its unpaved roads, and yet, compared with what I was used to seeing, in Bombay or even L.A., it did not look so dark. On market day, the streets were thronged with people snapping up manuals of 1986 Opals and copies of Tom Peters's guides to financial success, whole minivans and buses for sale in the giddy sunshine; at a time when the Prado, down below, was closed to traffic for the holiday, El Alto was so packed with cars and trucks that one could hardly move.

The growing stain of huts across the hill (which happen—such is Bolivia's freedom from conventional logic—to enjoy the best views in the city, all the way across the valley of light) is a sobering reminder of what happens when the country swallows up the city, and a ragged past comes to claim the present and the future. The walls around me, though not as furious as those in Lima, were inscribed with slogans hardly less poignant—"I do not believe that justice and equality exist," "We respect those who respect us"—and El Alto, thanks to the floods of rural poor hoping to redeem themselves in the city, has become the fastest-growing city on the continent. And yet it was hard, at the same time, not to be touched and warmed by the Ferris wheels and foosball tables that had been set out in the middle of downtown, or the sign (in the shape of a Christmas tree) up at the Internet café: THE THREE WISE MEN BROUGHT A SCANNER! It is often noted that Cervantes himself, father of Quixote, once tried (in vain) to be mayor of La Paz; and he, at least, might have rejoiced in the fact that even a massage parlor, in the national newspaper *La Razon,* offered an open-hearted message as the old year came to an end: "On the occasion of the coming of the New Year, the

Flor de Loto offers its distinguished clientele peace, happiness, and divine good fortune for the realization of all your dreams and plans."

The Bolivian, of course, seeing these same scenes, would see something very different. One day I stumbled out of my hotel, the Donald Duck cartoons it screened in its breakfast room for its pin-striped clientele still reeling through my mind (the front desk offered brochures for a "Museum of Play" on Calle Roosevelt), and, still a little woozy from the altitude (or from the gallons of coca tea I'd been drinking to offset the altitude), walked out into a demonstration. The whole central promenade—the present tense, as it had seemed to me at first—was taken over by block after block of ragged campesinos, shouting out their dissatisfactions. Every few moments, a firecracker of some kind would go off, the street would be rent with a thunderous explosion, and the Indian women, engagingly, would cup their hands behind their ears as if to protect themselves from the moment.

As I watched the banners marching past—THE ASSOCIATION OF JOYLESS WORKERS . . . GENERATION SANDWICH—a shoeshine boy came up to me and confessed his longing to go to America. To get rich, I assumed, or claim freedom, or at least to see Britney Spears. No, he said; he wanted to go and kill people in Afghanistan. His mouth was covered by a scarf, to protect him from the fumes of the traffic, and it wasn't hard to guess that he was one of the 35 percent of Bolivia's children who could neither read nor write. In the countryside, I'd read, some people did not even know how to put on clothes.

"It's so calm here," I said, thinking of the Lima I'd just come from, the Calcutta and Miami where I often find myself.

"Calm?" he said, and looked at me as if I was mad.

· · ·

For people who travel in search of the past, if only because the future is too much with them, Bolivia is a tonic place, with witch doctors walking up and down the street outside the San Francisco church. It is a country—like Laos, like Bhutan—that seems to have decided to go its own way, alone, and to hold to its traditions as some of the children I saw in the swelling market cling to the ponchos of their mothers. One day, near Lake Titicaca, I went to see a central church, and found a friar in a brown cassock, eyes tightly closed, sprinkling holy water over a long line of SUVs. Votive candles, bouquets of flowers, bottles of champagne stood before the lucky vehicles, and after they had been baptised and driven off to celebrate their beatitude, nothing was left in the little square but the smell of spilled bubbly, the stench of spent fireworks.

There are still ceremonial fights in rural Bolivia in which people are killed, and many young Bolivians are surely glad to be free of their parents' superstitions; but to the foreigner passing through, this often translates as a kind of sunlit antiquity. One evening, walking through the cobbled streets of the Spanish quarter after dark—the outlines of Indian women laboring up the hills, bags slung over their shoulders (with all the goods they'd failed to sell)—I walked down into the center of town, and into an aromatic mist. A long line of figures was gathered outside the entrance of the San Francisco church, and a young friar, busily chewing gum (or it might have been coca), was muttering prayers and placing his hands on the little cars, the miniature houses, even the dolls in baskets (representative of children at home or on their way) that were presented to him. Nearby, on the ground, slightly shabbier figures from the countryside waved sticks of incense up and down and promised more shamanic services, while little girls, caught up in the evening's merriment, snuck under the ropes that protected the church's crèche and came back, delighted, with replicas of the Virgin and of Jesus.

Left to practice its own rites in its own way, Bolivia had happily recolonized the past (the Spanish church made over with some highly un-Spanish ornamentation, put there by the Indian workers who had been forced to decorate the upper stories), and Epiphany (for that is what this was) had been translated into some local form. As long as the country could live on its own terms, and far from the world at large—and Bolivia seemed to sense this—some kind of rough peace was possible. But the foreigner is himself, of course, transporting a vision of the future to such places, and in our current global order, time is as violently thrown about as space.

For more than four thousand years the crop that has sustained Bolivia, in body and in spirit, has been coca, which, happily, can be harvested four times a year, or twice as often as rice and potatoes can. It is the way in which people on the Altiplano make contact with their goddess Mama Coca, daughter of Pacha Mama (or Mother Earth, as we might call her), and it is an integral part of weddings, festivals, and daily rites. When the Spanish came in and made peasants work forty-eight-hour shifts in the mines, chewing coca was also the way in which the locals got through the grueling hours in the thin air.

In recent times, however, as everyone knows too well, outsiders have found that coca can be turned into cocaine, and so, you could say, a religious prop and herbal sedative has been converted into a modern stimulant. Though one part of Bolivia surely protested this violation of its past, another shrewdly saw it as the future: in the 1980s, coca brought in roughly half of the country's export earnings. But when the U.S.—alarmed at the fact that its people, representing 5 percent of the world's population, accounted for 50 percent of its cocaine usage—found that it could not wipe out consumption at home, it decided to try to eliminate it at the source. Suddenly, Bolivians were told to forsake their ancestral crop because the affluent in New York and L.A. could no longer control themselves. In 1995, an American congressman actually vowed to drop herbicide on Bolivia's crops from airplanes kept on aircraft carriers "off the coast of Bolivia." Apparently no one had thought to tell him that the single most famous fact about Bolivia is that it's landlocked.

The day before I was due to leave Bolivia, having taken in all the other places mentioned in the guidebooks (the high, lonely emptiness of the Altiplano, as desolate as a pair of panpipes played on a quiet evening; the strange enigmas of Tiahuanaco, one of the great mysteries of the world, a few statues looking out on the unbroken plains all around, the sun casting huge shadows across the nearby hills; and the handful of tourists here—New Year's Eve—reduced to just stick figures in the distance), I decided to make my final attempt to see how Bolivia looked to the Bolivian, by going to the final site mentioned in my guidebook.

Just three minutes away from the Prado, where children were flying balloons and a merry-go-round, its cars shaped like the characters of Pokemon, was waiting to take them up into the air, there is a large building, on a street called Calle Canada Straight, that looks like an impregnable fortress. I slipped between two handsome buildings on the main street, mansions from the nineteenth century, and instantly was away from the commotion of the crowds, and in front of this building, the San Pedro Prison. Prisoners in Bolivia are required to pay their way through their years of confinement—the government, presumably, does not have enough money to support them—and one inmate, the guidebook explained, had decided to put together a living of sorts by offering visitors tours of his new home. The place was said to be a microcosm of the society around it: some people lived in "cells" that were as well appointed as five-star hotels, while others were squeezed, by the hundred, into spaces originally intended for twenty-five.

When I arrived at the prison, and the little park set across from it, there were only a few other foreigners milling around, most of them somewhat ragged types from Israel. I didn't know whom (or what) exactly to expect, and the other foreigners did not seem very eager to answer my questions, so I stood around with them and waited to see what the drill was. Suddenly a man came out and said, "Put your hands against the wall." We stood against the wall, and felt rough hands patting us down. Then we were told to stand there, in a line, and wait to be led in. Already the division between the innocent and the criminal was blurring.

We waited a long time in the hot sun and then at last two policemen came out and led us into a tiny, dark corridor, barred on both sides. A gate clanked shut behind us. In a courtyard—we could see through the barred windows—prisoners were everywhere, some standing in front of what looked to be a chapel, others wandering around with girlfriends or wives, or unpacking shipments from mothers, grandmothers.

A little boy was walking around the small space, his hand in his father's. The older man was looking down, as if distracted, and on a forced march. A young woman, pretty in T-shirt and new jeans, her tight ponytail swinging behind her, stood under a Sprite sign with her children, waiting for a husband or a friend.

As we looked out at the bleak situation, a man came up to the bars and started shouting to us in English. "Deny everything!" he said, as if he were a lawyer. "Deny it! If they find anything on you, just deny it! Don't give them anything!"

There was no room to turn in the narrow space, and the ear-ringed, shaven-headed Israelis looked no more comfortable than I was. We were pinned, all of us, in a space large enough for six, and every now and then a door would be opened, one figure would be led off, and then we would be one fewer. But it still felt as if there was no more room.

The prisoner outside kept shouting at us, and the armed guards who were in charge of us looked not amused at all at these tourists making their lives more complicated with a Sunday morning excursion. The whole expedition began to feel like a very bad idea.

As I waited there, with nothing else to do—the prisoner (a gringo, like us, who'd been found with drugs?) shouting advice, the guards patrolling the space outside our bars, occasional Bolivian families walking into the courtyard to check on their loved ones—I began to feel obscurely guilty: furtive and soiled. There must be something I had done, I thought, on which they could have me up; there were any number of irregularities of which I could be accused. The previous day, crossing a small lake in the countryside on a rowboat, I had come to a routine customs check—a little shack in the empty place—and the officers had taken away my passport. So now I was even less official, my formal identity taken away from me.

Around me all the faces I could see were hard, with scars. The gringo, himself disfigured, shouted and shouted as if in an asylum where it is only the sane who are taken to be abnormal. I began, as the minutes wore on, and nothing happened—the Israelis impatient, as I was, in our pen—to wonder if I'd inadvertently joined a group of real criminals, who were being brought in for drugs. After all, I had exchanged no words with them when I joined their group outside the prison; for all I knew, they were not tourists at all but suspects brought in for questioning of some kind.

What if someone planted something on me? Or if . . . ? Who knows what could get lost in translation?

I decided to get out. It was a difficult decision, and not a popular one, and the Israeli boys hardly made room for me as I tried to squeeze out. If coming to the prison on a Sunday morning as a tourist was a bad idea, suddenly deciding that you didn't want to come—after you'd brought yourself into a pen, a locked door behind you—seemed an even worse one. My fellow travelers snarled and muttered curses as I tried to push past, pressing themselves up against the bars in the narrow space.

"Is it going to be twenty minutes?" I asked one. "Do you know what's going on?"

He looked at me in disgust, and turned away.

When I got at last to the gate behind which we were locked, the guards looked at me as if I were a prisoner who had decided to let himself out. What did I want? they asked with their faces. I've decided to go home, I said in broken Spanish. Without a word, they pushed me into a tiny cell with a bare bed against one wall. There were two officers in the place, and barely enough room for anyone to move.

They motioned for me to strip, completely, and one of them started prodding my genitals with a truncheon. They motioned for me to empty my pockets, and I started taking everything out. My wallet, a comb, some keys. A pen, a handkerchief, a Japanese temple charm I carried around with me as protection.

My passport?

No, I said, I didn't have it here.

One of the guards picked up my small, inscrutable temple charm—a pouch with some characters in Japanese written on it—and, poking inside, found a piece of paper there. (I'd never known that the little pocket contained anything.) He took it out and began to sniff it. He unfolded it, folded it again, unfolded it. It contained a Buddhist prayer, I saw now, some words of good luck written out for anyone who purchased such a talisman. But the words were written in a language that none of us could read, and the guard continued looking at it. Why did I have this? What were these papers doing inside?

I looked around, and thought: who knows, but they could put something else inside the charm now, and then discover it. They could find anything they wanted, if they so chose, the way a tourist, confronted with sentences that he doesn't understand, draws the conclusions, makes the observation that suits him. The contents of my pockets—they might as well have been my entire life—lay scattered across the bed: a bronchial inhaler, a snapshot of a girl I know in Japan, the key to my hotel room. The previous day, at the customs shack, the inspectors had noticed that my height, as listed in the passport, hadn't been changed since I was a child. They'd looked and looked at me but hadn't been able to make out the childhood scar listed in the passport as a distinguishing mark.

"It's okay," a woman behind me in the line had said. "They think you're a terrorist." A few of the men who had flown the planes into the World Trade Center, I now learned, had been planning the assault while staying in cheap hotels here in La Paz, on Calle Saganagar. It was the perfect place to hide.

This morning, at breakfast, in deference perhaps to Camus's famous dictum—"What gives value to travel is fear"—I'd been reading Graham Greene's *Ministry of Fear,* an exploration of Kafka's themes which asks: Which of us, if suddenly brought before a tribunal, has an entirely clear conscience? Which of us has nothing at all to hide?

"Deny everything!" the man in the baseball cap shouted in the courtyard outside. "Give me the name of your hotel; I can get your stuff sent back to you. Deny it all, if they find anything on you." I'd taken him, before, for a friend, or at least the one person in the place who spoke my language; now I wondered what he was saying, and to whom.

"Rapido, rapido," said a policeman, as his friend sniffed again at the temple charm, truncheon at the ready. *"Rapido."* The other man began peeling back the soles of my shoes, first the left one, then the right. Out from my wallet came my credit cards, every banknote I was carrying. Out came my California driver's license, my business cards, the list of all my traveler's checks. Out came everything I had.

The excitement of travel, even in Bolivia, is that you're in a place where nothing makes more sense than in a dream: that pretty girl is smiling at you (or at the possibilities you represent), and the light above the snowcaps is exalting. Things have a sharpness in the high clear air they never have at home. The other side of travel is that nothing stands to reason: you've done nothing wrong, and now you're a fugitive, who looks very much like the ones who came here to bring down the global economy. The cops let me out at last and I walked back to my hotel just a few minutes away. I picked up *The Ministry of Fear,* and then put it down again. Somehow the appetite to read had gone.

The next day, I flew away from Bolivia, the Peruvian plane taking off (the Bolivian one having preferred not to at the last minute, as if to keep us here forever), and the whole place falling away from me, "like a shining bit of cold light," as a friend who knew the country had written to me, describing how nothing he had experienced in Bolivia translated to the world outside.

The plane rose up and up in the already high air (the airport here, as everyone always says, the highest in the world), and when I looked out the window, I saw the enigmatic towers of El Alto, standing sentry above the corrugated-iron shacks, the market that made a mockery of straight lines, the shantytown that went on and on as if to swallow up the broad streets and the high-rise buildings down below. Along the Prado those towers were standing as proudly as if on a southern Avenue of the Americas, their panes reflecting back the sun. Down below, in the southern valley, the condos and the gated palaces laid down in a straight row next to the rock faces.

But all around the straight lines, I could see now, from my aerial perspective, were lunar outcroppings, and wild rock formations that showed that this was where the city ended, and this was where the wilderness began again. In Bolivia, as in the California to which I was returning, the rich live very far from town, in places where people perhaps weren't meant to live at all. In California this meant scorpions occasionally in the kitchen, and foxes outside my bedroom door; mountain lions would surely take away the cat if the coyotes didn't. In Bolivia this meant sudden storms that turned the modern streets into rivers of debris.

And only then I remembered how, one glorious morning, in a state of high excitement, seeing the light knife-sharp above the mountains, I had hurried out of my hotel and jumped into a cab to go to the Valle de la Luna, the otherworldly collection of salt-colored pinnacles that forms a kind of alternative world ten minutes from downtown. I'd walked and climbed for an hour or more, up and down amidst the jagged peaks and stalagmites (as they seemed)—in and out of the unearthly pinnacles, the blue so sharp it took my breath away, and the whole place (this being Bolivia) deserted save for me.

I found a rough path leading up and over the upjutting rock formations, and each turn brought me into a new relation to the peaks, the billowing clouds so white it looked as if they would cry, the light reflecting off the far-off villa. A landscape of ash and rich blue, framed with light, and (I remembered from my previous, aborted visit) as soon resolved into a hailstorm blur.

I'd returned to the man who'd been kindly waiting for me— "Take as long as you need," he'd said, as Bolivians often do—and we'd gone back into the city, towards the skyscrapers. This was where the heliport was meant to be, he said, pointing to a space on top of a high-rise. These buildings were the future that had been so hopefully erected in the 1970s (before inflation hit a yearly rate of 28,000 percent).

We'd followed the decorated roundabouts into the very center of town—"Global Solutions" on one window, BMW showrooms and chic cafés—and arrived at what I'd taken to be the present tense. All around, though, I saw now (and I'd begun to intuit then), was a past so untamed and remote that just to walk around it for a few moments, ten minutes from downtown, was to feel that everything around me—the hotel, the lights I saw out of my window, the conclusions I was beginning to come to— was as fragile as the light, just turning now, beside the sunlit valley, to dark above the mountains.

2002

IN
THE
DARK

It was dark when I set foot on the island, and it felt as if the darkness was chattering. I could see oil lamps flickering at the edges of the forest. I could hear the gamelan coming from somewhere inside the trees, clangorous, jangled, and hypnotic. I could see people by the side of the road as I drove in from the airport, but I couldn't tell how many there were, or what they were doing in the dark. When I woke up, jet-lagged, in the dead of night, and walked down to the beach, figures came out of the shadows to offer me "jig-jig" or some other amenity of Paradise. There was a holy cave on the island, I had read, inhabited only by bats; there was a temple in the sea guarded by a snake.

The bush is burning only for those who are completely foreign to it, I had often thought; in the works of V. S. Naipaul, say, the jungle is seldom a force of magic, and if it is, it speaks for a magic that is only pushing back and down the clear daylight world of reason. Those born to nature seldom have to go back to it. Yet in Bali all these ideas are upended. Bali is a magical world for those who can see its invisible forces and read all the unseen currents in the air (that woman is a *leyak* witch, and that shade of green portends death). Yet for everyone else, it is simple enchantment. We stand at the gates of Eden, looking in, and choose to forget that one central inhabitant of the Garden is a snake.

I walked through the unfallen light my first day in Bali, to the beach, to watch, as foreigners do, the sun sink into the sea. Snake-armed masseuses were putting their things away for the day and boys were kicking a soccer ball into the coloring waves. As the outlines of the place began to fade, and the dark to take over, a woman came up to me and asked if I'd like to take a walk with her.

I couldn't really see her in the dark, and the name she gave me—Wayan—is the same name given to the oldest son or daughter of every family on the island. It was pitch-black as we walked along the sand, and pitch-black when we turned into what I thought was the little lane that led back to my guest house. At night in Bali, the dogs come out, and they are nothing like the serene creatures who sit outside the temples of Tibet, seeming to guard the monks. The dogs in Bali howl and curse and bite. As we walked through the forest on the path back to where I slept, I could feel the dogs very close to us, and everywhere.

We know Bali, those of us who read about it, as a magic island where there are thirty thousand temples in a space not much bigger than a major city; we have heard that it is a forest of the kind you see in *A Midsummer Night's Dream*, where people fall in love with the first Other that they meet. A childhood friend of mine had had her first experience of real transport with a stranger in a thatched hut on Kuta Beach; all around, you can see what look like asses—or rude mechanicals—waiting to be picked up by Titania.

But the stranger by my side did not seem interested only in romance as she led me up into the heart of her island's cosmology of light and dark. We walked along the buzzing lanes of Kuta after dark, dogs growling on every side. We walked along a beach on the other side of the island, where couples are supposed to walk on full-moon nights. We took a ride up into the interior, where whole villages are given over to ritual dance: small girls were fluttering their bare arms in the temple courtyards, and boys were chattering in a trance. Foreigners often awaken in the night in Bali to see ghosts standing by their beds; when a brother needs to communicate with a brother, a Balinese dancer once told me, with no drama in his voice, he finds telepathy easier than the telephone.

I walked through all these spaces with the girl from the beach, and through the skepticism I brought to them, and felt at times we were walking through parallel worlds: she could read everything around us, and I could read nothing. This was the way people were buried on the island, she said; this was why black magicians lived in that forest of monkeys. Part of the excitement of being a foreigner in a place like Bali is that you can't reduce the signs around you to an everyday language.

That is also what is unsettling about being a foreigner in a place like Bali, and after some days I slipped away from the girl, and went to the airport, to fly away. When I got there, she was standing at the gate, come, she said, to say goodbye. We would not meet again, she went on, because she had dreamed the previous night that she would put on a white dress and go across what is the Balinese equivalent of the Styx.

This is the kind of mystery that makes an almost ideal souvenir: something strange and a little spooky that you can take back to your regular life in (as it was for me then) Rockefeller Center. When I chanced to return to Bali, eighteen months later, I took pains not to tell Wayan I was coming, and to make my way discreetly back to the little lane where I'd stayed before. But when I came out of my guest house the first night back, at dusk, there she was, waiting, at the threshold, as if we had made a prior arrangement.

We went out again into the dark, the unlit fields behind the night market, the lanes that seemed, after dark, to be inhabited only by dogs. It was better to meet in broad daylight, I told her, and made a date to get together on the public beach at noon. She was wearing a sky-blue dress when I met her there, not scarlet as before, and her manner was withdrawn. I wasn't here for very long, I said, I didn't know where we were going: all the visitor's easy evasions. She looked at me, and then it was goodbye.

When I went back to my little room, I was unable to move. For days on end, I couldn't stir. I wasn't feverish, and yet something in me was waterlogged, leaden. I couldn't step out of my hut to eat or drink or take a walk; I couldn't sleep. For three days I lay in my bed and listened to the dogs amidst the trees, the gamelan. An Australian was pressing his claim on a local girl in the next room and she, laughing, was dancing away. I saw lizards on the walls of my room, and I awoke one morning to find that the lizard was nothing but a light switch. I went up into the hills, summoning all my strength for the one-hour trip, but something in me was evacuated: a guardian spirit vanished in the night.

It was time to leave the enchanted island, I decided. But before I did, I wanted something to remind me that I had been here, and that all of this had really happened: proof, of a kind. The streets of Bali teem with masks, which hang from the fronts of stores, staring-eyed, with tongues protruding, as talismans of the island's nighttime ceremonies. Knowing that they were too potent to take back home, I looked for something more innocuous, and found an owl.

I took the owl back with me to my small studio apartment in Manhattan and put it up on my wall. Almost instantly the New York night was so full of chatterings and hauntings that I had to get up and rip the thing down, and put it away in a closet where I'd never have to lay eyes on it again. You go into the dark to get away from what you know, and if you go far enough, you realize, suddenly, that you'll never really make it back into the light.

2002

ON
THE
ROPEBRIDGE

If you turn off the main road that leads from Gyantse to Shigatse, in the central Tibetan province of Tsang, you come, very soon, to a dirt road that bumps through fields of barley, and over a couple of small streams, to a small, green-roofed monastery tucked against the mountains, out of the sight of passing traffic. A few children are playing in the muddy streets, and their voices come up to greet you in the quiet morning. A yak (or maybe it's a *dzo*, a cross between a yak and a cow) is standing stationary under the high blue sky. The thin air gives the whole plateau a sense of unnatural illumination, so you feel, as you pass through late-summer fields of wild mustard, as if you are not yourself, light-headed, prone to dreams.

The monastery is seldom visited these days; it belongs to a small esoteric order that is not part of any of the four major schools of Tibetan Buddhism. It was never as much a target of Mao's Revolution, therefore, as are the more famous temples around Lhasa, and though it has seen its share of damage, it remains inhabited by the past in a way that few of the more familiar temples do. Almost the only adherents of its doctrine are the people who live nearby, their square houses sitting near the main road, as in a pueblo, earth-colored, with blue-and-white awnings fringing their windows, and decorated curtains. Women in long turquoise braids labor up the steep, thin ladders that connect one floor to the other, and up above, as everywhere in Tibet, prayer-flags flutter in the wind, carrying their messages up and up.

As I jangled along this road, one day in the rainy season of 2002, I ended up at a small entranceway with only two dusty cars and a bus outside it. Inside, through a low gate, was a central courtyard where two young monks, in red, were seated at a folding table, as if selling tickets to a high-school prom. I handed over some banknotes—quite a few—and one of the boys got up, pulling his robes about his shoulders, and motioned for me to follow him through a low opening into the next courtyard, and a prayer hall. Inside, like all the chapels of Tibet, it was dark. Candles flickered in the little rooms that led off from the main chamber, and the air was thick and dark with the smell of melted butter, the dust, the incense of centuries. Through the gloom I could see a few faded murals, and as I wandered among the chanting figures I slipped, more than once, on ground made uncertain by years of melted yak butter.

This day, as it happened, the handful of monks who belonged to this order had arrived from every corner of Tibet (hence the bus) to partake of a special ceremony. They sat now in long rows, on cushions on the floor, the light flooding in from the small high windows in shafts, and muttered low, sleepy chants in the dark room. At one end of a row, on a slightly raised chair, sat the young head of the monastery. Around him, tired, dusty, shaking monks, not reading their sutras from books, as is usual in Tibetan monasteries, but reciting them by heart. Eyes closed, bodies rocking back and forth on their cushions, the whole room seeming to shake and tremble with its collective, ragged chant.

I knew, from two previous trips to Tibet, that there was nothing very otherworldly in this gritty, embattled place. People lived here as they had always lived, as if to vindicate Camus's assertion, based on his native Algeria ("There is a solitude in poverty, but a solitude that gives everything back its value"). In the old days of Tibet, so easily romanticized, when a quarter of the population was said to be attached to monasteries, this meant that the great temples were great political forces in their own right, with armies and strategists and enormous monk policemen. Now that the temples served different purposes, as Potemkin tools of the government in Beijing, many of the monks who remained were said to be informers or spies, luring foreigners to say a little too much about their feelings for the Dalai Lama, or listening for real monks who cursed the Chinese presence.

As I stood in the uncertain light, a young monk hurried up and down the lines, pouring tea into rows of little cups from a heavy silver kettle; another was wandering around with a sleek new digital camera from Japan, turning the long rows of red-robed figures into smaller, tidier rows on his compact screen. Around us, amidst the protective deities and icons, were pictures of the Tenth Panchen Lama in various lives; the most prominent pictures featured him sitting with a motley dog in his lap.

Tibet is not an easy place to live, and as I listened to the low grumbles, wishing for long life and peace for all sentient beings, I noticed that many of the monks had lesions on their feet, or even deformities. Some were inordinately fat, some so thin it seemed they would evaporate altogether. They were a very ordinary group of people, living in conditions of great poverty, and trying to find some hidden compensation in their ancient, changeless chant.

As I looked up and down their lines, however, my eye stumbled on a single tall figure seated in the back row. He sat perfectly erect, hands cradled in his lap, head straight, though his eyes were closed, and it seemed as if he were sculpted out of light. His posture was impeccable; he sat, among his fellows, somehow apart, in his own realm, entirely transported. He never moved as he murmured his chants, and it was hard not to think of a statue of the Buddha, lit up somehow by a candle inside.

My guide gestured for me to come out into the sun with him, and we drifted away. I looked back at the gathering as we left and saw this solitary figure, almost alone among the monks, seeming to sit in a corner of light, the hands in his lap cupping fire. Then we were out again in the high, strong sun, and climbing up a ladder into another courtyard of chapels, where my guide, drawing from a huge jangle of keys at his side, opened one door, and then another. On the walls of the old place were whole diagrams of the universe, the stench of years, or centuries, of smoke and melted butter. Gods of compassion and protection; pictures of staring-eyed lamas and the magician who gave us much of what we know as Tibetan Buddhism, Padmasambhava. Here and there—the monk pointed with his hand—the judge who consigns souls to the realm of light or to that of dark, a figure surrounded by skulls.

We stood in the dust and silence of several centuries and then went back out into the sun, and returned to the main prayer-hall just as the morning prayers were ending. The neat lines of monks had broken up into a cluster, and as the assembled gathered in a group to go to lunch, I went and stood as close as I could to the one I had picked out. He looked back at me and raised his palms together in greeting. His eyes were unnaturally bright, and his face was clear. Then, returning his attention to the other monks, he joined the great mass of them as they proceeded down the long hallway, chanting as they went, under murals that had been here for almost a thousand years.

We went out again into the sun. An old monk, helped along by two attendants, raised a cupped palm to me several times, in the traditional Tibetan gesture of welcome. Then I got into the car again, and bounced back towards the main road, and five minutes later we were driving towards Shigatse.

What exactly you believe, and how much, and why, is a question Tibet asks you more searchingly than any place I know. It's part of what travel involves everywhere—the stepping out of the bounds of what you know, and into the realm of wishfulness and illusion and real marvel—but in Tibet it comes with centuries of legends, and a self-consciousness, on both sides, you don't find in other cultures. We go to Tibet, often, to be transported, and so, inevitably, we are (as we might not be if we saw and heard the same things in Wisconsin); "Tibet" is the name we give to whatever we wish to believe, or can't quite credit.

In the modern country, of course, this dovetails with the other central question of travel, which is how to put the terrible conditions you see around you together with the radiant sunlight (stronger, sharper, closer to the heavens in Tibet than in any lower place). The Chinese would say that the issues are related: Tibet is poor precisely because it devotes its time to gods and prayer and superstition. Many Tibetans might reply that karaoke parlors and industrial cranes look to them like what is truly barbaric. The traveler, anxious in most cases to see the particular beauty and dignity of an ancient culture preserved—yet in no position to suggest that its people live without the schools and hospitals he finds so essential himself—walks between the two sides as across one of the ropebridges that famously span the gorges of the Himalaya. Swaying one way, as the wind catches the bridge, swaying the other.

When I arrived in Tibet on this particular trip, one week before coming upon the hidden monastery, I experienced what might be called the reverse of déjà vu: I couldn't believe I'd ever been here before. The streets, the shape, the very skyline of Lhasa were transformed beyond recognition; where once there was a scramble of old houses at the foot of the Potala Palace, now there was a theme park, with swan boats and an old airplane, where people could dress up in Tibetan finery for the duration of a photo. China, as is well known, has brought Tibet into the age of enlightenment with broad streets and high-rise apartment blocks and department stores; the result is a city that looks like an Eastern Las Vegas, one unnaturally fat strip of huge discos and modern hotels set in the middle of what would otherwise be lunar emptiness. CHINA MOBILE banners flutter from the lampposts of the wide, spotless boulevards, and a billboard presents you with a picture of Deng Xiaoping, Jiang Zemin, and Mao Zedong, beaming beside the Potala (the same Potala that Mao, for one, showed every sign of wanting to destroy). It's as if a glossy propaganda poster had been laid down on what was once a jumble of family snapshots.

When first I visited Tibet, in 1985, just after the country opened up to the world at large, I came upon a festival of hope and light: Tibetans delighted to see the foreigners who seemed to belong to a different universe from theirs (as of 1979, fewer than two thousand Westerners had been to Tibet in its entire history); travelers just as astonished to find themselves in a "Forbidden Kingdom" that had not even seen wheeled transport when we were young. Flower boxes shone in the blinding sun outside the whitewashed houses, shy monks came out from their prayer halls to toy with my camera, and at night the few of us who'd managed to steal into this secret enchantment went up onto the rooftop of our rickety guest house to watch the Potala under the full moon, its thousand windows alight.

By the time I returned to Tibet in 1990, all the lights were out. Martial law had been declared after Tibetan monks (spurred, perhaps, by the foreigners who gave them now a voice, a contact with the world) began crying out for independence and human rights; soldiers patrolled the rooftops of the low buildings around the Jokhang Temple, the holiest site in Tibet, and tanks were parked nearby. Tibetans were not even allowed to visit the Potala that is the center of their culture, and every morning they stood plaintively at its gates, watching the few tourists who were in evidence led around the magnificent symbol backwards. Even those of us who were admitted were led through a largely shuttered place, scarcely lit, its doors closed, where often the electricity went out altogether and we were left in an absolute darkness.

Now, coming back to Tibet, I found the passage across the ropebridge shakier than ever: the place was neither festival nor blackout. On the one hand, the temples were filled with Tibetans, eager to throw themselves in front of the sacred statues and crawl under dusty scriptures in the hopes that wisdom, or at least grace, would be passed down to them; on the other, the pictures of the Dalai Lama that once flooded the altars were replaced by those of the small boy Beijing has chosen as the

Eleventh Panchen Lama (the Tibetan choice still under house arrest, as he has been for seven of his thirteen years). The Tibetans I met seemed much less put out than were foreigners by the gleaming new buildings full of boom boxes and signs for Giordano and Jeans West, but one day, as I sat in the middle of an ultramodern street, taking its wonders in, two friendly Tibetan matrons came over and looked at the real source of wonder in the area: the pen with which I was transcribing the scene. The little guest house where once I shared a single cold-water tap in a courtyard and a foul-smelling hole in the ground with thirty or forty others now offers a sleek rooftop restaurant where you can eat Japanese and Mexican food and where Jim Morrison sang (the night I visited), "This is the end, my only friend, the end . . ."

A foreigner, flying into Lhasa on one of the six China Southwest planes that go back and forth every day from Chengdu in the summer ("California Dreaming" streaming through the cabin, and video monitors screening an antic Hong Kong gangster movie for the mostly Chinese passengers), may try not to notice the PETRO CHINA sign that greets him on arrival; the air-control tower that says, pointedly, THE LHASA AIRPORT OF CHINA; the teams of tour groups from Beijing piling out in zippy "Discover Tibet" baseball caps. And yet as I walked around the Potala, a young Tibetan came up to me and said quietly, "For view, beautiful"—I was looking out of one of the small windows to the city below—"but what for human rights?" As I wandered around the central market—rows of monks everywhere, rocking back and forth on the ground over their chants—the monks extended their hands, and when I declined to give them anything, sneered in a highly unmonastic way. Sitting by the reflecting pond that the Chinese had built outside the Potala, I found two little girls, no older than six or seven, clambering over my lap, running hands over my face, cooing, "Give me money. Give money."

In many of the chapels in Tibet now, it costs $20 just to use a camera, and in some of them $250 to turn on a video camera; the scatter of old buildings that had made up most of Lhasa when first I visited was now called "Old Town," as if it were an artificially reconstructed area in a yuppie suburb. I thought sometimes, in the evenings, of the place that had so moved me when I had first come, put me on the rooftop of my being, as it felt, and opened a kind of window so a high clear light came through; I'd never been to a town that took me so far from everything I knew. Then I thought of the Dalai Lama, asked not long ago by a colleague of mine how he regarded the discos at the foot of the Potala. "No problem," he said, "no problem," implying that such surface changes were not important, provided that something more fundamental, in his people's souls and stomachs, was respected.

Because of its location, behind the highest mountains on earth and two miles above sea level, and because, too, of the isolation in which it has been left, seeming to pursue not material development, as you could say, but immaterial, Tibet has always attracted visitors of a certain kind, and they, like every kind of visitor, have usually found, or claimed to find, exactly what they were seeking. Monks who run two hundred miles at a stretch, in a trance; others who can raise their body temperatures just through the intensity of their meditation. Monks who can levitate—seem to fly—and others who have perfected the psychic skills that have left Madame Blavatsky, Gurdjieff, Paul Brunton, and a host of notorious others transfixed. It all sounds highly implausible until you think of how a Tibetan villager might respond to the news that Americans have walked on the moon, that people can speak to one another across the globe on little wireless instruments they carry in their pockets, or that the Chinese god "Wang Dao" (or Michael Jordan, as we call him) can be seen flying over a basket ten feet above the ground.

I picked up a copy of *Magic and Mystery in Tibet* while I was staying in Lhasa—the young Chinese student sitting across from me in the sunlit courtyard of the Yak Hotel (black T-shirt and long ponytail) was deep in a copy of *Lost Horizon* himself—and tried to orient myself to Alexandra David-Neel, who greets the man who sets out her itinerary for her, in the book's opening paragraphs, as "a genie come down from the neighboring mountains." Like many a Himalayan adventurer, perhaps, she seemed to have few qualms about offering her wisdom to the Thirteenth Dalai Lama ("the Omniscient," as she calls him), or about exclaiming, at one point, "Oh, to talk with this magician who shot avenging cakes through space!" It wasn't entirely surprising (or reassuring) to find that the author was depicted in a frontispiece wearing a rosary of "108 circlets cut out of 108 different human skulls" and wearing at her waist a "magic dagger" and a "kongling trumpet made of a human femur."

The introduction to the Frenchwoman's accounts of her early-twentieth-century sojourns in the Himalaya, by a member of the Académie Française, called the excited wanderer a "complete Asiatic" while noting that she "remains a Westerner, a disciple of Descartes," committed, in her way, to what others have called the empirical study of another world. Yet reading her stories of men who must "practise the uttering of *hik!*" to free the spirits of the dead, or the *delogs* who have "returned from the beyond" in Tibet—seeing that her eagerness to be transformed ran ahead, perhaps, of her intelligence ("It was difficult to begin a conversation with the ascetic, as his mouth appeared to be full of rice")—I couldn't help but recall T. Lobsang Rampa, the enigmatic author of *The Third Eye* and other books of Tibetan magic, who turned out to be an unemployed English plumber who'd seen the virtue of branding himself as a Tibetan. "I don't like this place," the token scientist says in the movie *Lost Horizon,* as his companions start settling down amidst the five-star comforts of Shangri-La. "It's too mysterious."

I remembered, too, as I read of the Frenchwoman's fascination with occult or magical practices, the Dalai Lama, asked if he could remember previous lives, shrugging and all but saying, "Perhaps, but what's the point?" It would be a kind of stunt, he suggested, that would have nothing to do with leading a better or more attentive life. David-Neel's dressing up as a Tibetan seemed most apt insofar as she referred to "the habitual Tibetan mixture of superstition, cunning, comedy and disconcerting events."

And yet, driving in from the airport a few days earlier, past great statues of the Buddha carved into rocks (and obscured now by tour buses, flying cameras, and children hanging on to visitors' shirts, crying out, "Give me money! Give me pen!"), I'd seen the friend I brought to Tibet suddenly lose all color in her face. "I dreamed all this," she said quietly, as if not wanting to be heard, "a month ago." Later—though never given to such presentiments elsewhere—she was convinced she saw the face of her long-lost brother in a statue in the hidden monastery, and in Shigatse, an image of Avalokitesvara seemed to smile at her. When she flew away from Tibet, having suffered through days of diarrhoea and headaches from the altitude, and having been unable to move often, from mysterious ailments, she said that she felt cleansed somehow, able at last to embark upon a new chapter in her life.

Sitting in California, in the comfort of the sun, I'd put the conundrum of Tibet into a neat diagram on my desk. On the one hand, there was a culture (China) that had consecrated itself entirely to progress and to profit, and had decided, following the god of consumerism, that whatever was new was good and whatever was clean was right. On the other, there was a culture that asked how much going forwards was actually a matter of sitting still and to what extent progress meant, in fact, a passage backwards, into the ancient and the deep. It was the same dialogue that one hears in many a household (or many a heart), the old folks saying, "Things will never be as good as they were when we were young," while the grandchildren say, "Things will never be better than they are tomorrow." One group pulling you to one side of the swaying bridge, one group to the other.

As soon as I began walking around Tibet, of course, such simplicities dissolved: the two worlds are woven around one another so tightly that you can't tell where one ends and the other begins. At some level, the two worlds live parallel identities in the same space: Tibetans, for example, walk around all the holy places clockwise, while the Chinese, out of defiance or just ignorance, walk around them sometimes in the opposite direction, as if to reverse the spell. Tourists (who are mostly from China these days) ascend the Potala from the back, and then walk down through its rooms backwards, from top to bottom; Tibetans ascend along the front of its sheer white face, following the zigzagging patterns of what they call "the pilgrim's path," and going from room 1 to room 2 to room 3. Besides, Tibetans visit the building in the afternoon, while tourists go in the morning. The "People's Park" that the Chinese celebrate around the

Dalai Lama's Summer Palace is still for Tibetans the Norbulingka, or "Jewel Park."

And yet things are rarely kept so conveniently apart. Many of
the sweetest people I met, in Shigatse and Lhasa and elsewhere,
were, in fact, the Chinese settlers—shopkeepers and taxi drivers
from Sichuan province who had come here to make the new lives
they could not find at home. (When I'd visited before, I'd felt
saddened and outraged at what the monks and other protectors
of Tibet had to endure for their belief in freedom of religion and
speech; but it had been hard, too, not to feel sorry for the Chinese soldiers, often, teenage boys, clearly lost and far from home,
put out by the altitude, thousands of miles away from the government that was inflicting on them this duty, and surrounded
by people famous for their powers of resistance.) In some sense,
too, part of the Chinese policy is to blur the distinctions between
the cultures through intermarriage, and to flood the area with
so many Han that you can no longer talk of a separate Tibet.
Besides, the power of the land has never been unequivocal: the
writer of the major guidebook to the area, I heard, on coming
back from Lhasa, had been found by local nomads in a cave, gib-
bering like a madman, and had to be shipped home.

For foreigners, inevitably, much of the magic of Tibet lies in
the fact the place is so undeveloped. Around the Barkhor, the
traditional pilgrim's circuit that also comprises Lhasa's central,
age-old marketplace, you see figures from the farthest reaches
of human experience. Pilgrims whose faces and clothes are en-
crusted with black, and who have walked two thousand miles
or more to visit the holy city, sometimes prostrating themselves
every step of the way. Wild men from Kham, tassels of red
strung around their hair, and others who stride around with ceremonial daggers. People sticking their tongue out at one another
for hello in the ancient Tibetan way, and, inside the Jokhang

Temple, in the dark, lit up by butter-lamps that throw a strange light into their faces, countrywomen singing folk songs as they prostrate themselves before an auspicious statue. All day and into the night much of Lhasa is a constant murmur of sacred chants and shuffle of prostrations, as locals fall to the ground again and again, stretching themselves out in honor of a culture that is fast dying and a leader who is long gone.

I mentioned once to the Dalai Lama how moved I had been by the fervor and the absolute devotion I had seen in Tibet, more intense than any I had seen in any culture of the world. He looked surprised. "That's just blind faith," he said, as if wary of giving too much credit to what does not stand up to science or to reason. I told him another time how moved I had been by the Tibetan spirit, and he said, "What good is spirit if there's no Tibet?"

We live, the psychologists (and our intuitions) tell us, in two domains at once, and if we move too much to the side of either one, we run the risk of falling over the ropebridge and getting picked up and carried away by the rapids down below. Those who travel out of modern secular societies, as the great explorer of religions Huston Smith points out, are often going in search of ancient cultures that are, as often, looking back at them. The result is that both parties find something other than what they think they're looking for, the nomad in his yak-hair tent against the mountains stumbling upon an Itagelato restaurant on Beijing Dong Lu (as it's now called) in Lhasa, the visitor so opened up that the smallest thing can set him off.

The one time, before Mao, that a sizable group of Westerners came into Tibet all at once was at the end of 1903, when Colonel Francis Younghusband led one thousand British soldiers (and more than ten thousand coolies) to Lhasa, to see if they could form an alliance of sorts with the Tibetans. In "Great Game" terms, Tibet, an area as large as Western Europe, had always been strategically charged, with its openings onto Russia and China and India. No one was very taken aback when Britain's viceroy in India, Lord Curzon, decided to send an expeditionary force to Tibet, partly on the flimsy grounds that Tibetans had been attacking Nepali yaks across the border.

As Younghusband's troops moved towards the capital, they succeeded in slaughtering 628 Tibetans in less than four minutes near a village called Guru, many of the bewildered locals shot from behind as they walked in consternation away from the battlefield, protected only by charms decorated with the Dalai Lama's seal. Later, at another site near "Red Idol Gorge" (as the British rendered it), almost 200 more Tibetans were killed, while British casualties amounted to three wounded. At every point the invading troops, as they seemed, fired on the locals with machine guns, and the Tibetans retaliated with slingshots or flung rocks. Though the British gamely carried wounded Tibetans to a military field hospital, the overall impression, in John Buchan's words, was of a "big boy at school" pushing back an "impertinent youngster."

When the British arrived at last in Lhasa (the Thirteenth Dalai Lama having fled), they marched through its streets with their Gurkha band, and crowds of Tibetans clapped. Younghusband congratulated himself on his reception, not knowing that clapping is how Tibetans try to expel evil spirits. And after concluding a typically inconclusive treaty with Tibet's regent— the Barkhor by now had been dubbed "Piccadilly Circus," the Potala, "Windsor Castle"—Younghusband, on his final night in Lhasa, took a ride into the mountains. Suddenly, he was overcome by an overwhelming mystical vision of peace. "Never again could I think evil or be at enmity with any man," announced the bluff British soldier. "All nature and all humanity were bathed in a rosy glowing radiancy." Before long, back in London, he was setting up a World Congress of Faiths, speaking up for Indian independence, and writing mystical books like *The Gleam*, in which the visionary Indian who catches a glimpse of eternal life is, in fact, a depiction of himself.

All this fits into the standard mythology of Tibet. And yet the real story is even more mysterious. As it happens, Younghusband had been drawn towards the place across the mountains long before he entered Tibet; as he sat on its plains preparing for battle he steeped himself in Whitman's *Leaves of Grass* and books on "Cosmic Consciousness." Going out from the camp in cold so severe that ink would freeze immediately, he began writing out in pencil what he hoped would be a volume on "The Religion of a Traveller." And in all his journeys, he felt that the exploration of remote places was really "an exploration of the very heart and soul of things, the discovery of the real Power, the inner Being, of which the outward facets of Mother Earth's face, the plants and animals and we men, are but the expression." According to his biographer, the house in which Younghusband's parents lived, in, of all places, Dharamsala, is now perhaps the one occupied by the Dalai Lama's younger sister.

In Lhasa, as the days went on, I took to going out very early in the mornings to see Tibet reclaim itself. There were no Chinese visible—almost no tourists—at four or five in the morning, and so I would go out of my room in the Yak Hotel, down into the courtyard, the sound of early buses and late taxis in the blue-black streets outside, and try, almost literally, to steal out of my confinement. The Yak Hotel was guarded by a huge gate that was bolted in the night. Next to it sat a Chinese soldier at a guard post. Often, though, when I went out, the man was so fast asleep that I was able to take the keys from his side, unlock the bolt in the gate, pull back the great bars, return the keys to his side, and go out into the chill and bracing street without his noticing.

The alleyways were pitch-black at this hour; my feet, as I fumbled across the mud, sometimes lurched down into a puddle, or slipped on something less than solid. Few figures were visible then, and those that were were merely silhouettes: a little old woman, walking around the Jokhang very fast, spinning her prayer wheel furiously as she went; a strutting man from Kham, so exuberant at his early-morning circumambulation that he was shouting out prayers to the sky.

Girls swept the small area in front of their stalls or shops. A lone monk sat on the ground, a robe covering his head like a hood, and recited his prayers in a steady, muttered chant. As I walked around the central temple, at one point, in the distance, the Potala came into view, high up, on its crag, though unlit these days, even at night. The building that once presided over the city, visible from every corner, is now only caught in snatches here and there.

In front of the Jokhang are two stupa-shaped white furnaces, and as the sun began to rise above the distant mountains, and light to leak into the sky behind the temple, old women, often, would push cyprus or juniper branches into one of these caverns, and pour gasoline all around. The temple was soon flanked by two burning fires, and much of the square became a juniper-scented mist out of which pilgrims and visitors appeared, and then disappeared as abruptly. Somebody put on a radio—a crackle of folk songs came on—and even the little stall that called itself the "Jokhang Square Control Office" was shuttered in the early morning.

Immediately in front of the temple is one little chamber reached by descending a few steps slippery with melted butter. In it were just lines of lamps with tiny candles inside. As the sun appeared above the temple, the door to this underground place opened, and a few Tibetans went in and began slowly, patiently, putting a light to each in the long row of lamps, the lights casting an unearthly glow back into their faces. From afar the temple began to seem a fortress with small, flickering candles lined up in front of it.

From farther back, one could see the billboard that had been erected in the square, saying, pointedly, in English, NATIONAL CULTURE ALSO BELONGS TO THE WORLD. Next door, one of the only guest houses run (for many years) by Tibetans had a gold plaque at its entrance: EXEMPLARY SITE OF SPIRITUAL DEVELOPMENT IN TOURIST INDUSTRY. In front of me, the rows of candles flickering in the near-dark.

The single item that has done most to fix in the world's mind the notion of a magical, and indestructible, Tibet, not subject to the laws of other countries, is of course *Lost Horizon.* "Welcome to Shangri-La," announces the paperback copy that I picked up in Lhasa (THE FIRST PAPERBACK EVER PUBLISHED! the cover also says), and on the back I read of a place "high in the distant reaches of the Tibetan mountains where a group of worldly men and women have stumbled upon a land of mystery and matchless beauty, where life is lived in tranquil wonder, beyond the grasp of a doomed world." In Frank Capra's movie of 1937, this faraway kingdom, which seems to be a corruption of the legendary Tibetan sanctuary of Shambhala, is described, in an opening storybook frame, as "a place where there was peace and security, where living was not a struggle but a lasting delight," and one so far from our notion of civilization that it remains nothing but "a blank on the map."

In both the movie and the book, the creators of Shangri-La take pains to make their vision concrete with wry and ingenious details. A bathtub in the never-never land features the trademark "Akron, Ohio," and the mysterious lama Chang, in James Hilton's account, "observed the social formalities of Bond Street." The hero, Robert Conway, is a sometime Oxford don (another "disciple of Descartes," perhaps, and a classic British gentleman who has always been drawn to "the other side of the hill"), who, trying to find ways to explain Shangri-La, even to himself, confesses that it's "a bit like Oxford." All five of the newcomers arriving in Shangri-La have good reason to want to settle down there, and one (a former criminal) actually comes up with a scheme to introduce plumbing to the benighted people.

The author is also careful to frame the story of Conway's flight into the Himalayas with accounts of the men he'd left behind him sitting in their London club, discussing him. The last words of the book, pinning down the very earthly time and place of its composition, are "Woodford Green / April 1933."

And yet the most bewildering thing about *Lost Horizon* may be that this syrupy romance, loved and derided by generations in all its incarnations (the book, the movie, the restored Capra movie, and then a remake, starring Liv Ullman) proved, in fact, more clairvoyant than any of its makers had a right to expect. In the movie, the High Lama—living in a Tibetan palace that looks suspiciously like a movie mogul's mansion in Bel-Air (and is now, in part, a luxury spa not far from my home in Santa Barbara)—prophesies a dreadful war and a man equipped with unprecedented weapons of destruction. Four years after the movie came out, America was at war, and eight years later Oppenheimer and his colleagues launched an atomic bomb upon the world. The High Lama's repeated motto is, simply, "Be kind," a slogan that would seem simplistic indeed were it not the same concrete, easy-to-remember message that the current Dalai Lama takes around the world to people from cultures very different from his own ("My religion is kindness"). The governing principle of Shangri-La is "moderation," even to the point of forbidding "the excess of virtue itself," and that sounds too good to be true until you remember the Middle Way that is the talisman of many a Western Buddhist today.

Most of all, the central action of *Lost Horizon*, in which some fallen, squabbling souls end up, because of war, in a long-unvisited kingdom run by lamas, actually came to life ten years after the book was written, when a rough-and-ready Austrian mountaineer named Heinrich Harrer escaped from a POW camp in India, with his friend Peter Aufschnaiter, and stumbled by mistake into Tibet, where he fell into an idyllic world out of time, as it seemed, and became a close friend of the teenage Dalai Lama. Five years after the movie was shot, a U.S. Air Force plane really did crash in Tibet. One of the only foreigners the book imagines as stealing into Shangri-La is, as it happens, an Austrian soldier who keeps the lonely holy man company. Even the details in the film that seem most purely (impurely) Hollywood—flocks of children, surrounded by deer, singing Brahms's "Lullaby"—aren't entirely absurd when you remember that pipers in Tibet in the old days played "It's a Long Way to Tipperary," and four Tibetan boys, early in the last century, were sent to be educated at Rugby, in England.

When two Hollywood movies recently told the true story of the Fourteenth Dalai Lama (re-creating Lhasa and the Potala Palace in Argentina and Morocco), *Lost Horizon* was mocked as a quaintly naive vision of Tibet from a time when almost no foreigner had been there (its High Lama, famously, a European priest, more than two hundred years old, who is hoping for "the Christian ethic" to prevail). And yet the world in some ways has begun to catch up with Hollywood's much discredited vision. In 1987, the Dalai Lama suggested Tibet be protected as a "Zone of Peace." (In the book, Shangri-La functions as a zone of peace in which people are free to "stay with our books and our music and our meditations.") In exile, the Tibetan leader has also said that China's occupation has reminded Tibet that it cannot afford to ignore the present. ("We must move with the times, you know, even in Shangri-La," says Hilton's Lama.) When Hilton's hero hears the great man expound the history of Shangri-La, he is moved, for the first time in his life, to fall to his knees; one turn of the Tibetan (or the Chinese) calendar later, when Heinrich Harrer and Aufschnaiter really did stumble upon the prospect of the Potala, "we felt inclined to go down on our knees like the pilgrims," Harrer wrote, "and touch the ground with our foreheads."

As Lord Gainsford, in the St. George Club, says at the end of the movie, after having spent ten months trying to keep Conway from returning to his dream, "I believe it because I want to believe it."

My very last morning in Tibet, just hours before going to the airport, I suddenly awoke violently. It was still dark outside—the prayer-flags that crisscrossed the space around my room were just triangles fluttering in the blackness. The rain had subsided an hour or two before, but when I looked out of the window to the soldier sleeping at his guard post, I could see it was still misty and damp, very close to rain. I sat against the pillows in my bed, and, anxious to go to sleep, began to write. Page after page, unstoppably, though writing was the last thing I wanted to do at

4:00 a.m., before a long day of traveling that would take me to Chengdu, then Guangzhou, then Osaka, then Los Angeles.

I thought of the temple I had visited off the dirt road—the monk sitting stock-still, in his cupped glow (I can see him even now), so much like a statue of a Buddha that he seemed a symbolic representation of sorts. I thought of the light fading over Tashi Lhunpo Monastery in Shigatse, the last few monks returning to their rooms, the sound of chants from an upstairs room, a lone elderly monk, like a policeman, walking up and down the lanes to make sure that everyone was home now, and safely behind locked doors.

I thought back to all the moments that had most haunted me in Tibet, and started writing about winter afternoons at my school in England when the lights would come on in the little cobbled lanes, and one could hear boys reciting their verses for chapel, or class in the morning, and the black-robed forms disappearing in the mist or suddenly materializing, in a town that had not changed, one could imagine, for centuries. Soon there would be prayers—all of us lined up in our unbroken rows—and not long after, at dawn, more prayers, and old monks, as they seemed, watching over us. Now there was just the cold of evening, and unheated rooms, and the damp, the chill, that still prevailed in all the fifteenth-century rooms.

The next day, when I was gone from Tibet, I dreamed I was back in Oxford, the town of my birth, and boarding a bus I lost my wallet, all tokens of my identity. I opened a book to learn more of the monastery I had seen, but I could find no mention of it anywhere. It wasn't included by name in *Magic and Mystery in Tibet*, though it seemed home to precisely the esoteric practices celebrated in that book; it wasn't listed even in *The Tibet Guide*, a compendious description of Tibet's temples and their icons compiled by the scholar Stephen Batchelor. I sat in my room at home, and thought back to the signs for a "Lhasa Satellite Conference," and the banners across the street (often obscuring the Potala) that said PARADISE OF DREAM SEEKERS. Then I thought back to a shaven-headed young monk, eyes closed, utterly unmoved by everything around him, and I wondered if the "real Tibet" could ever be destroyed, insofar as it is something, for resident, exile, and visitor, that lives mostly in a place that can't be seen.

2002

GRANDMOTHERS

Sometimes, from my desk here in Japan, I see boys in the park across from me, hitting and hitting a ball with a large blue baseball bat. Their grandmothers sit in the sun, on benches, the leaves turning gold, russet, above them, and then coming down around them like confetti. A woman sits by herself on another bench, sketching the colors in front of her, and a flock of Boy Scouts is sent to gather all the trash (nonexistent, as far as I'm concerned), their yellow shirts fluttering across the clean green spaces.

I walk across the park, on a narrow path at its edge, in the autumn sunlight, and feel a foreigner's sense of wonder: the convenience stores placed along the small, shiny road, as if they were just more vending machines; the two-story houses, tidily guarded by their walls, lined up along the narrow streets like salarymen in their business suits waiting in a receiving line for the future. Every trace of the old expunged as efficiently as once the trees and the rice paddies were, here in this place where hope means the West, and tomorrow.

All this, I know, is foreign only for a foreigner: the kids around me, in their hip-hop gear and surfer shorts, regard baseball as a Japanese invention, as Japanese as that McDonald's outlet down the street. ("Did you see cannibals?" Africans ask one another when they come back from Europe, Ryszard Kapuściński writes.) Yet just a little behind the sleek new stores, at the edge of the neighborhood, where the streets run out, there is a deeper foreignness that is foreign even to the native: deep gulleys, often, or slopes of trees uncut. The visitor steps up to the wild space, and then steps back, and retreats to the shiny machines he knows and trusts.

I go sometimes to the local train station—banks of TV sets broadcasting all the cable channels of the world onto its platforms—and take a ten-minute train ride. When I get out, at the final stop, I step into the celebrated Deer Park, an open space so large and wild it takes up the entire center of the ancient capital, much as the Imperial Palace does in Tokyo, and its ghostly predecessor still does in Kyoto. A large silent space that exists near the center of the place the way something may be just near the heart of a person, seldom seen, but still essential. In its absence, there'd be nothing.

By day the park, running all the way from the station, the noisy arcades, the high-rising department stores, to the hills, is generally full of tour buses, schoolchildren brought here on a tour of their collective past, foreigners anxious to see the last untouched part of old Japan. But as soon as dusk descends, the place empties out, and, walking towards the hills, I can feel as if I'm the only person in the world.

A couple, perhaps, is peeping through a fence at the great Buddha temple, said to be the largest wooden structure in the world. A salaryman is walking, jacket over his shoulder, past the white-globe lanterns, home. A foreigner extends his arms, a temporary king, under the high ceremonial orange *torii* gate, built for ghosts and giants.

Otherwise, there is not a trace of anyone. I follow a stone path deep, deeper into the woods, the dark, and all noises, all commotion fall away. There are only deer, on every side, coming out onto the path after nightfall, as if to reclaim their territory. Ears cocked, noses alert, standing, stock-still, amidst the trees to see where I am going. Occasionally, a great gust of them—thirty or forty or more—takes off in a silent canter, then disappears into that farther darkness.

The deer, aggressive in their demands for food by day, are perfect Japanese hosts at night. They don't come close to me, they don't step away. I walk towards the flight of wooden steps that leads up to a temple on the hill, and they simply stand on every side of me, attentive. On the gravel path, amidst the trees, behind me in the dark: waiting for the trespasser to leave them to their home.

A few months from now, a festival will be held that dates, they say, from the time when Nara was the Buddhist capital, thirteen centuries ago. Men in white robes run along the terrace of the great temple on the hill, which overlooks the city, and the torches they carry shake in the night, and make the wooden building seem to tremble. The runners place, with great fanfare, the torches on the edges of the terrace, and sparks rain down on all the beings who have collected below, many of whom scramble in the darkness for auspicious ashes. Again and again, silently, the men carry their torches across the platform—gold streaks across the blackness—and send stars scattering below.

The deer stay quiet for the duration of the festival, wait patiently in the trees for the crowds to pass. After ten or fifteen minutes of gold-running, the crowds disperse, back to the station, hugging themselves in the cold, rubbing mittened hands together. You know, the old ladies tell the smaller beings beside them, that the deer are sacred messengers; they bring us news of the gods, who live somewhere in the hills.

An automated voice announces the next express train, and the teenagers with yellow hair pour in from the pachinko parlors and the bars. The visitors go back to their homes, and the deer step out again in the dark.

The people all around me on this shiny autumn morning, refulgent and cloudless—though the trees are beginning to turn, and today, for the first time, we put on thicker sweaters—are the very old, the very young; the others are off tending the fires of official Japan. I walk across the path in midmorning, and see old ladies walking with canes, out to get exercise as the leaves come down, or, as often, with tiny creatures by their sides, pointing out to them the cosmos flowers, that dog in winter coat. The very old and the very young live on the edge of things—though they're central in Japan—and are closer to the woods; they don't have to go and check in on the daylight world. They can talk, or make up stories, about the creatures still known as *kamisama* here, or nature's gods.

The grandparents weren't such good parents themselves, perhaps, when they were young; but nature is affording them a second chance. They have time now—in the short term—and freedom, while it lasts, to pass on whatever their grandparents passed on to them. To tell the toddlers at their side that the fox who waits at the edge of the trees isn't really a fox at all; to say that that stranger who sits in a frame on the shrine isn't a stranger at all, but their grandmother's grandmother. The children, lost in their own games, don't bother to say that there isn't a picture of any old woman on the shrine at home, and they know the foxes they see on TV aren't real. That's what makes them special.

They listen, because that's what they're supposed to do; perhaps they nod. And, being natural lawbreakers, they tell their grandparents a thing or two, about what that animal is saying to its owner, and what the secret name of that tree is. Their fathers are seldom visible, and their mothers are chafing against the uncertainties of a world of 7-Elevens and feudal rites; but the deer, the badgers stay the same.

When I was the same age as the children in the park, innocent of school (innocent, as it happened, of ghosts, though not of autumn leaves), I was asked to take a small part in a local production of *A Midsummer Night's Dream*. Oxford is often known as the center of England's largest motor works—Great Britain's Detroit, if you like—but in one corner of the industrial city, Neville Coghill, the distinguished scholar of Chaucer, and friend to C. S. Lewis and Tolkien, summoned the dormant spirits of the soil to life and asked them to resume their pagan duties. Spirits flitted through the trees of Worcester College, and the Queen of the Fairies took her leave of men by drifting across the college lake. Puck danced from corner of the night to distant corner, and the ghosts of ancient Greece, which Shakespeare had brought into a sylvan evening in Elizabethan England, jumped across the centuries again and walked among us.

I saw the *Dream* again last night, in Nara, on a rented video from the Tsutaya Culture Convenience Club, and wondered if the scenes would seem strange to my neighbors in the park. Even the young, in their backwards baseball caps or their Chanel, go to shrines here where the temple charms are sold to them by women dressed in white, as vestal virgins. They walk around the pond and look at the *O-tsuki-sama,* or—in the kind of honorific translation that used to make us laugh when we were young— the "Most Honored and Godlike Moon." They address the heavenly body, in fact, almost as Pyramus and Thisbe might in the Shakespeare play.

I walk into the park—the light is failing now, the evenings are coming early—and I think the boys playing baseball would have no trouble believing that fairies could put spells on us so we fall in love with the first person we see upon awakening. Gods make sport with us here as if we were living in ancient Greece (or modern India).

Every morning, in my home, my Japanese companion rings a bell and lights a stick of incense in the shrine she's made next to her Panasonic boom box. She closes her eyes, says something very fast—or nothing at all—and I remember how, when first I met her, I took her to an amusement park, and she came out of the haunted house genuinely shaken. Ghosts are real to her; behind the flashing lights of Japan is something dark, and very old.

I look at all this strangely; growing up, I had no grandparents within several thousand miles of me, and took that to be liberation, a chance to make my own future (even to choose my own past—I could take my gods and elders, the global order told me, from Japan as much as from my ancestral India). Those born into the modern world are free, at times, if they are sufficiently comfortable and sufficiently modern, to make their own sketches of their futures, as their grandparents never could (though what they actually draft on their blank pieces of paper sometimes looks surprisingly close to what they would have drawn through inheritance).

And yet in Japan, walking around the park in the autumn light, everything blazing, and about to pass away, I wonder what it means to get one's grandparents, one's ghosts, vicariously (because one is missing grandparents and old wives' tales—missing, in effect, those pieces of collected wisdom passed down from age to age that we laugh at even as we're secretly committing them to memory). We go, some of us, to places where we can live, for a few weeks, by candlelight; we pick up a novel by a Chinese woman in San Francisco who reports that her mother saw the whistling of the wind as a wailing from her old nursemaid in Shanghai, many decades ago. Gods and ancestors are all mixed up in the old cultures—where grandmothers may be taken, as much as deer, to be messengers from somewhere else; a belief in ghosts, the shrine by the boom box says, is just, in effect, a way of having faith in what you can't actually see.

One morning when the blue above me is immaculate, I go out and, past the long line of tearooms and souvenir stores in the center of town—glove puppets sold in the shape of Buddhas and deer—come to a small wooden gate that leads into a shy, largely forgotten temple. A white board—high-rises on all sides—tells how the temple remembers the time a deer stole in, a thousand years ago, and ate a piece of calligraphy. A young monk, seeing the intruder, threw a stone at it, and the deer collapsed. The monk, though only thirteen himself, was condemned to death, by Nara custom, for slaying a messenger of the gods. Now, the stone turtle in the temple garden asks people to pray for the boy, who would otherwise go unmourned.

When I return to my apartment, the light still radiant, my partner tells me that she just went out to see her closest friend, and the woman, hardly older than herself, held her and held her, and said that they would never meet again. She'd been diagnosed with cancer, in its final stages.

My friend silently lights her stick of incense, and rings a bell, over and over; her eyes remain closed long after the bell stops ringing.

Outside, the days turn and the leaves come down. The people in my neighborhood change their futons, pull out heaters; autumn brings festivals in commemoration of the old, and of the very young. Winter will bring a whole other set of rites, and colorful occasions whose meaning has been forgotten, but whose observance continues amidst the video games and robots. People do things because they do things here, the way we used to sing hymns in church: indeed, autumn makes the least of us philosophical, even if our philosophy never evolves, but just says the same thing every year. And the saying of the same thing becomes part of the pattern of the world, its natural shape.

I walk down the street and wonder if a large part of the human enterprise isn't just the task of fitting ourselves into the larger order, adjusting to a scheme that will roll on and on long after we have been replaced by someone else. In England, when I was growing up, we thought of life as a play, a performance of some kind in which we were given a script at birth, asked (quite politely) to play our part as convincingly as we could, and then told (no less politely) to retreat gracefully and make room for someone else. This can mean—it usually does mean in Japan— fitting oneself into a social order, a family, a community, a com- pany. But for those of us who choose not to be a part of that—to be permanent foreigners, you could say—it means only reconcil- ing ourselves to, and around, the larger cycle. The woman who was sitting at my dinner table a few weeks ago, in the prime of health, is about to die. The last warm days are about to pass until they return again, five months from now.

One virtue of grandparents, of seasons, or deer who come down from the hills, is that they remind us that we don't know everything, and can't make the world up entirely from scratch; much of it—most of it—is beyond our reach, even beyond our reckoning. In the larger view of things, available to grandparents and ghosts, trivial things have fallen away, and important things never change.

Only the old, in some sense, are in a position to appreciate this, and to see what the young can bring with their reviving freshness. And that lady who sets up a spirit-house on her lawn in West Hollywood is telling us, without a word, that we can all of us save time by remembering the lessons of those who've gone before us; a large part of who we are isn't very individual at all.

One day I pick up Ryszard Kapuściński's most recent book on Africa and read that the elephant, on what is said to be the oldest continent in the world, is treated as a sacred animal, in part because he has no enemies, and also—so the legend has it— because he never dies. He just gets exhausted and walks into a lake, never to be seen again. His death is never seen or talked about; in that sense, it never happens, or is regarded only in the invisible world. I read such things—I've never been to the country Kapuściński is describing—and feel I'm hearing news from a distant radio station I can hardly catch.

Then I think of the deer, not far away—the area in which I live is called the "Southern Slope of Deer"—their ears cocked, their eyes watching from the trees, to protect the territory that is their own. In Oxford, at the college where I studied—the college I'd visited often as a small boy, growing up in the city—there was a deer park, as near where the Buddha taught, and forty or so animals walked among the elm trees beside the buildings where professors held their weekly tutorials. The deer were protected from us by a fence, but we could touch them through the gratings, and always see them as we went to classes, or back again, to plays.

It was said that the number of deer must always match the number of Fellows in the college, leading to an easy joke about what might happen every time a deer died. And once a year, in the autumn, some of us were invited to a great feast of venison when, for whatever reason, the number of deer had to be brought down. I didn't know the meaning of the phrase "tutelary spirit" then, and even if I had known it, I would not have paid heed to it or stopped to think what it might connote: now, however, half a world away, I think of what happens when the darkness falls on Nara Park, and almost nothing is visible but the nighttime outline of the great temple and the stone steps leading up into the dark. Outside the temple, in the emptiness, you can see the large stone guardians taken from China as emblems of protection; everywhere else, the deer, stepping through the trees.

2002

THE
FOREIGN

"It was as if a world of neat
hollow squares and snappy
counter-marching had deteriorated
into rout or mindlessness."

—GODOLPHIN, *an eccentric*
British explorer in
Thomas Pynchon's V.

NIGHTWALKING

I fly and fly, across the largest ocean in the world, over ice floes or tropical islands, far from any season I know, and get out in an airport that dissolves all sense of time and place. Long corridors, panels of glass, screens above every door, clicking over. Men in suits disappearing down this escalator, appearing from that one, drifting away along that moving ramp.

I walk and walk as if across a screen myself, and at another gate, more men in black waiting to disappear into a hole, a stranger comes up to me and says, "Excuse me. Are you Pico Iyer?" I don't know what to say, but the safest answer seems yes, and he places a book of poems in my hands, stands beside me as a flashbulb pops, and then is gone again.

We go up into the sky once more—six miles above the earth now, and darkness everywhere—and when we descend, a few hours later, the pilot welcomes us to Ninoy Aquino International Airport, named after the opposition leader who was killed on this very tarmac not long before. The night is dark, and my body, up now for twenty-five hours—or forty, by my watch—is full of life, ready to walk out into the morning.

I get into a car and we drive down Roxas Boulevard, sudden fireworks of silent lights around the gaudy discos and the karaoke parlors, and then the dark returning all around. I put my things in a hotel and go out again, with a new-day briskness, to get my bearings in this foreign place. Men appear in front of me talking about this girl, that club. Music thumps out of a darkened doorway. Faces are peering out at me as the door opens, and as I take shelter in a beer garden (2:00 a.m. now for the people around me, eleven in the morning for me), I see rats scuttling under the chairs where young girls, alone, eyes closed, are singing last year's love songs.

I get up and walk, to ground myself, to try to imprint on my floating mind something solid and substantial, and as I do I pass a young girl, sitting up abruptly on the sidewalk, and starting to pass a comb through her long, straight hair. She couldn't be more than twelve or thirteen, and yet she gets herself ready for bed as if in a Manhattan duplex, and then lies down again, on the street, and pulls a sheet of cellophane above her.

Around her, all around, whole families are sleeping. Children are huddled on the main divider of the street, and parents, with clothes like mine, who look as if they expected a future not so different from mine, are stretched out in careful patterns beside the streaking taxis. I walk among these outstretched figures in the dark and another woman smiles out at me from the bushes. She is very young, and very pretty. She says how warm it is tonight, how lonely. She smiles at me in the dark.

I walk and walk, to try to get back what I knew this morning (or was it last night? Two days ago?), but whatever I thought I knew has been effaced, by everything around me. In the casino on the main drag—3:00 a.m. now—there are so many bodies I can hardly move, the lights from the chandeliers catching the excited faces as figures press and shout above the spinning wheel. I step out and go exploring in the beauty salon next door, climbing the grand staircase of an old colonial mansion, and finding, at the top, girls recumbent in the hair-cutting chairs, too poor, I assume, to have real homes in which to sleep. In one room, no less mysterious, a Japanese boy lying flat out on a treatment table, a young woman coming in now and then to adjust the sheet above him, his feet protruding beneath it.

On the street again, by the cloud-covered ocean, the first fathers and their children are beginning to extend their fishing rods over the water as the sun comes up and the traffic begins to intensify behind them. In the grand hotel down the road, which remembers Marcos and MacArthur, sweepers are making the halls impeccable and uniformed workers pass through the dining room like ghosts. The first elderly couples are out now in the park, whole clusters of them, skittering, the women flashing their bright skirts like tropical birds as they practice ballroom dancing.

I go back to my hotel, ready for a good night's sleep—it's coming on for 9:00 a.m.—and when I awaken again it's dark, the traffic beginning to subside outside my window, the roar of the vacuum cleaners outside my door long gone. The streets are beginning to empty out as I go out into the dark, the men, the women beginning to congregate in the shadows. But everything is less strange now because I know the routine in some way, half expect that whisper behind the trees. Very soon I won't make out the people sleeping in the streets. The shock of the poverty will have become part of the daylight world for me, something I could easily take for granted.

In my regular life—the one I call "real"—I go to sleep every night at eight-thirty. My body gets me up as soon as it is light and by the time darkness falls I'm starting to lose consciousness, fast. All the corners of the night, therefore, everything associated with the sleeping world, is as foreign to me as Antarctica. In my regular life I know the time so well that I can tell the hour to the minute without looking at my watch.

Under jet lag, however, all that is thrown into convulsions. Not just the steady routine, the sense of clear divisions, the ability to get on with the world, in synch with it. No, something deeper is dissolved. I get off a plane, seventeen hours out of joint, and tell naked secrets to a person I know I don't trust. A friend starts talking about her days—her plans, her friends, the things she wants to do—and tears start welling in my eyes, in a restaurant. I can't sleep at night (because I've been sleeping in the day), and so I try to go through my routine, as I might in the daylight world. But I write the wrong name on the uncharacteristically emotional letter. I shower the stranger with endearments. When the lady at the bank offers me a $3,000 credit for the $30,000 cheque I've given her (a large part of my yearly income), I smile and say, "Have a nice day."

I often think that I've traveled into a deeply foreign country under jet lag, somewhere more mysterious in its way than India or Morocco. A place that no human had ever been until forty or so years ago, and yet, now, a place where more and more of us spend more and more of our lives. It's not quite a dream state, and yet it's certainly not wakefulness; and though it seems another continent we're visiting, there are no maps or guide-books yet to this other world. There are not even any clocks.

I live these days in Japan, and my mother, who is in her seventies, lives alone in California. Every time I want to look in on her, therefore, I get on a plane and take the ten-hour flight across the Pacific. But for a week—at least—after I arrive, I'm not myself. I look like myself, perhaps, I may sound something like myself, but I'm wearing my sweater inside-out and coming out from the unremarkable movie *Bounce* very close to tears. I'm not the person I might be when I'm antic or giddy or have been up too late; I'm a kind of spectral being floating above myself.

Every time I fly back to Japan, I become the meridian opposite of that impostor, a Sebaldian night wanderer who can't be trusted to read or write anything for at least another week. If I visit my mother four times a year, therefore—a reasonable thing to do in the ordinary human scheme of things—I spend eight weeks a year, or almost a sixth of my life, in this nowhere state. Not quite on the ground, yet not entirely off it.

A day, a human day, has a certain shape and structure to it; a day, in most respects, resembles a room in which our things are ordered according to our preference. It may be empty or it may be full, but in either case it is familiar. Over here is the place where you rest (10:00 p.m. to 6:00 a.m., perhaps), over there the place where you eat or work or feel most alive. You know your way around the place so well, you can find the bathroom in the dark.

But under jet lag, you lose all sense of where or who you are. You get up and walk towards the bathroom, and step into a chair. You reach towards the figure in the other bed, and then realize that she's seven thousand miles away, at work. You get up for lunch, and then remember that you've eaten lunch six times already. You feel like an exile, a fugitive of sorts, as you walk along the hotel corridor at 4:00 a.m., while all good souls are in their beds, and then begin to yawn as everyone around you goes to work.

The day is stretched and stretched, in this foreign world of displacement, till it snaps. I sleep, and sleep again, and the dreams that come to me, suddenly and violently, seem to belong to someone else. A Buddhist scholar (whom I've never met in life) is talking to me about transience, I'm talking of a house burning down, I'm slipping into a back room at a wedding with a long-ago girlfriend. Every one of the dreams, I realize when I awake, is about the dissolution of self.

Of course it is, my more settled, sensible self will tell me, your sleep itself is jangled. You've been hurried into the next room of consciousness before you've had a chance to pack. You're falling into unconsciousness in the middle of a sentence, with the TV on, and all the parts of you undigested.

And yet, somehow—such is the state of the spell—I can't hear this voice in the place where now I find myself. My stuff has been stolen—and stolen again—and I am suddenly bereft. A woman is speaking perfect English to me (though we are on the streets of China), and I know, somehow, that she speaks like this because she grew up in Fiji. A parade of ladies of the night walks past, and the woman, in a Chinese café, asks me what I should do about my stolen things.

When he was a boy, I recall, Rudyard Kipling awoke one night with a start, and realized that he'd been walking in his sleep. All the way through the dreaming house and out into the garden, as the light came up. "The night got into my head," he wrote, and soon thereafter became the laureate of Empire's troubled subconscious, all that happened on the dark side of the camp.

I go out again, as obscurely proud as a child who has climbed Everest before breakfast, and greet the figures streaming off the boat—it is Bangkok now, 6:00 a.m.—as they go to work. Vendors selling chili with meat, or mint leaves, and, on the far side of the river, monks paddling from home to home in the early light. At each house built above the water, a woman bends down to give the monks an offering of vegetables and rice.

The last taxis slipping back towards the suburbs. The girls finally leaving the discos and clubs and heading back to the shacks where they sleep across the river. The city caught by surprise, going about its private rites while the bulldozers, churning, in the little lanes, all the neon now turned off, grind back and forth, back and forth, removing the evidence of night.

Because jet lag is so much a part of my life now, I tell myself I will make the most of it—attend to it, enjoy its disruptions, as I would those of a geographically foreign place. When I return to my mother's home, therefore, I go out at first light for lunch, and enjoy seeing my hometown as I have never seen it before: the smell of kelp above the fast-food stand, the pungent tang of the sea that will disappear once the day is under way. People returning from parties, or the graveyard shift, others going out into the day while it is still virgin: all the people I never see in my ordinary life.

And when I return from California to Japan, I return by way of some strange Asian city—Kuala Lumpur, Shanghai, Hanoi— and, for my first few nights of discombobulation, prowl the dark. Were I to go to anywhere that resembled home, I'd be keeping everyone up by going out for lunch at 3:00 a.m.—and would, in turn, be thrown out by them as I turned in for a good night's sleep at eleven in the morning. So, embracing the traveler's first rule—everything is interesting if you look at it with the right eyes—I use the sleeplessness to try to see a world, a self I would never see otherwise.

I step out of the airport in Singapore, though in Singapore it's easy to feel as if you've never stepped out of the airport: everything is so spotless, so streamlined, that the entire city feels as if it's a line of duty-free stores, and man-made rain forests, set along landscaped streets. A visitor always feels he's on a tour bus in Singapore, even if he's alone—being guided around the sights of the "Singapore Story" film that is screened for tourists at the airport round the clock.

Under jet lag, though, another city comes forward, as if the twenty-first-century construct were peeled away to reveal something more odorous and ancient, less domesticated. The last few tubes of pink fluorescent lighting are still on in Little India, where the women sit on rattan chairs in evil-smelling doorways and look out into the dark. The temple pythons who guard the unmarked alleyway, and offer good luck, are gone now for the night, but the joss sticks still burn beside the candles in the Chinese shrine. The vendors sell potency pills and dildoes from their wheelbarrows. Groups of men circle around, muttering, pushing one another about, and now and then, in a bout of intoxicated courage, one of them steps forward, into the room, and states a price.

Along the shiny malls of Orchard Road—the new, official Singapore, where Barnes & Noble and Marks & Spencer and Nokia and Nike all share a single entrance (there's a Starbucks on this intersection, a Starbucks on that one)—tall girls who weren't girls when the day or the decade began flounce outside the Royal Thai Embassy, walking up the sidewalk, walking down it. The only other figure in sight is Ronald McDonald, seated on a bench, one arm extended, surveying the outlines of what seems a burger paradise. Farther down, along the water, the faces of Manchester United and Chelsea follow me as I walk along a strip of bars, their neon lights reflected in the canal. African men are disappearing down a street of bobbing red lanterns, where the international phone-call centers have the overbright clarity of provincial police stations.

I see a woman, standing at a window, arms folded, in a long black backless dress, staring out into the night, and then, coming round, I see that it's a mannequin. A White House official is reading from a text about the war on an oversized screen above the steps that lead down to the disco called Underground. Outside the clamorous bars of Orchard Towers—Crazy Girls, Sex, the Ipanema World Music bar—the taxis are lined up, forty strong, and the waitresses smiling at you as the doors of Country Jamboree swing open are all wearing ten-gallon hats. It could be Singapore, of course, but it very likely isn't.

The lure of modern travel, for many of us, is that we don't go from A to B so much as from A to Z, or from A to alpha; most often, we end up somewhere between the two, not quite one, not quite the other—in an airport, perhaps, that is and isn't the place we left and the place we think we're coming to. Jet lag, in some ways, is the perfect metaphor for this, the neurological equivalent, I often feel, of some long grey airport passageway that leads from one nowhere space to another. It speaks, you could say, for much in the accelerated world where we speed between continents and think we have conquered both space and time.

And yet, of course—this is its power—it isn't just a metaphor. It's painfully real, as real as those words that are coming out slurred, or that piece of paper on which we've methodically added 2 + 2 and come up with 3. We've been placed at a tilt, and the person that comes out from us is someone suffering from something much deeper than the high-frequency hearing loss or the super-dry sinuses that flying six hundred miles an hour above the weather in a pressurized cabin mean.

Being human, we try to counteract the spell in the usual human ways, by exchanging secrets and telling stories. Take leopard's bane, or melatonin; walk barefoot across fresh grass for ten minutes after you arrive. Carry a fluorescent light box with you to reproduce the patterns of the place you've left; turn your watch forward as soon as you board, to the time of the place you're going to.

But none of it, I think, really speaks to the person we're becoming. I feel, when lagged, as if I'm seeing the whole world through tears, or squinting; everything gets through to me, but with the wrong weight or meaning. I can't see the signs, only their reflections in the puddles. I can't follow directions; only savor the fact of being lost. It's like watching a foreign movie without subtitles, perhaps; I can't follow the story, the arc of character, but something else—that inflection of a hand, this unregarded silence—comes through to me intensely.

Things carry a different value, a different heft, when you're jet-lagged, but there's no counter on which the exchange rates are posted. People will tell you it's like being under a foreign influence, but it's not; for one thing, unlike with drink or drugs, its effects don't diminish with the years, but grow and grow. You can make rules for yourself for what you should do in this parallel world, but they are rules, by definition, you can't remember when you need them (the imagination is a drunk who's lost his watch, as Guy Davenport says, and has to get drunk again to find it). Once, under jet lag, I threw away all the notes I'd taken on a magical, and unrepeatable, foreign trip. Another time I decided to do my taxes just off the plane and, happily ignoring a $40,000 credit, faced month after month of I.R.S. letters and threats.

I try to make the most of it, as ever, and say that jet lag can release me from the illusion of the self. Getting off the plane, I go through three months' worth of correspondence, and hardly notice that this letter is praising me to the skies while that one is condemning me to perdition. They all belong to someone else, I tell myself, and I'm very happy not to be a part of his drama.

The next day, trying to pick up the pieces of my life, I go out to the post office, the bank, and all I can see is a desperate loneliness in the faces in the street; they seem plaintive, unclaimed somehow, as if they were issuing a cry for help. For someone who's just stepped off the plane from Japan, where everyone wears a mask of cheerfulness as she goes from one place to the next, it's all unnaturally unnerving.

The next day, though, I've begun to settle into the world around me; I hardly notice the lonely faces. Four, five days later, if you were to remind me of what I'd said before, I'd say, "What are you talking about? Everything's normal. These people are just the way they're supposed to be."

One day in 1970, a woman called Sarah Krasnoff made off with her fourteen-year-old grandson, who was caught up in an unseemly custody dispute, and took him into the sky. In a plane, she knew, they were subject to no laws; and if they never stopped moving, the law could never catch up with them. They flew from New York to Amsterdam. When they arrived, they turned around and flew from Amsterdam to New York. Then they flew from New York to Amsterdam again, and from Amsterdam to

New York, again and again and again, for the better part of six months.

They took 167 flights in all, one after the other. They saw twenty-two different movies, an average of seven times each. They ate lunch again and again, and turned their watches six hours forwards, then six hours back. The whole fugitive enterprise ended when Mrs. Krasnoff, aged seventy-four, collapsed, the victim, doctors could only suppose, of terminal jet lag.

I wake up one day in my mother's house, on one of my periodic trips "home," and we have breakfast together. She walks more slowly than she used, and has lost, she tells me, two inches in height; now, as I prepare to fly back across the Pacific, she shows me the articles and clippings she's saved up for me. A cartoon from *The New Yorker*, an article about the virtue of drinking water eight times a day.

She drives me to the airport, bravely, hardly letting on that she might be sad that her only living relative is flying to the far side of the world, only putting out a protective hand as I disappear through the security machine. I get on a small propellor plane for Los Angeles and see her standing at the gate, waving. At seventy, there are certain things you must let go of.

I watch her standing there, waving and waving as the plane starts up, begins to taxi, then takes off into the heavens, and I know that this is an image I must keep close to me. A person for whom I am responsible in some respects, too kind to burden me with her own concerns.

Fourteen hours later, I'm on a different continent, and hardly able to imagine the life, the home I left this morning. It's as if I've switched into another language—a parallel plane—and none of the feelings that were so real to me this morning can carry through to it. It's not that I don't want to hear them; it's that they seem to belong now to a person I no longer am.

Was it always like this, I wonder, when people were just boarding carriages for London? Or, even today, when a nephew of a friend of mine makes the two-week-long walk to school across the fields in Kenya? Isn't infidelity part of the sales tax, part of the lure, of travel? It is, of course, and it's nothing but the nighttime side of the dissolution of self, the release from normal boundaries that flight induces. Indeed, it's part of what moves us to take flights in the first place: to walk through that archway of lights and become a different person. A girl in a long dress is serving up an elixir of forgetfulness. The music numbs us into a kind of trance state. Lethe—the Sirens—is available on every corner in the global order.

And yet the man who disappears into the dark arcade knows at some level what he's doing, and chooses the amnesia that's waiting for him. He drinks to forget, he goes home with a stranger explicitly because he longs to escape the life that doesn't satisfy. In the realm of jet lag, though, the double life feels accidental: you're watching TV and someone comes up and changes the channel on you and you can't summon the energy to get up and change it back. I don't want to betray the life I left behind six hours ago, but I've changed my money on arrival, changed the voltage on my shaver, and I'm working in a different currency now. I could take a drug of sorts to reverse the effects of the drug of displacement, but I'm not sure if it could return me to the person I was when I got on the plane. All it could do, perhaps, is induce me to forget that he is someone different.

"You'll call me when you get there?" a sweetheart asks.

"Of course I will," I say, and do. But whoever is calling isn't the person who made the promise, and the sentences, the sentiments, so achingly alive last night, sound as if they're coming from someone else.

Not long ago, in Damascus, I lived for a few days on muezzin time: long silent mornings in the Old City before dawn, walking through labyrinths of dead-end alleyways, in and out around the great mosque, and then long hot days in my room sleeping as if I were in my bed in California. Then up again in the dark, the only decoration in my room a little red arrow on the wall to show which direction Mecca was.

I went on like this for a while—watching the light come up in the mosque, seeing the city resolve itself into its shapes in the first hours of light, and then disappearing myself, down into a well—and then, after a few days, something snapped: at night, by day, I could not sleep. I stayed up all the way through a night, and the next day couldn't sleep. I drew the curtains, got into pyjamas, buried myself inside the sheets. But my mind was alive now, or at least moving as with a phantom limb. Soon it was dark again, my time to wake up, and at last, at 2:00 a.m. or so, reconciled to my sleeplessness, I picked up an old copy of *Fear and Loathing in Las Vegas* and began to read.

From outside, in the fourth-floor corridor, the sound of a door being opened, then closing. Furtive rustles, a circle of whispers. The thump of a party, forbidden booze, female laughter. The ping of the elevator as it came and opened its doors; the sound of the doors closing again, the machine going up again and down. Sometimes I went to the window and, drawing the curtains, saw minarets, lit in green, the only tall monuments visible across the sleeping city. Once, putting away the story of Dr. Thompson and his Samoan, I opened the door to check the corridor, but there was no one there. No footsteps, no figures, no anything.

Hours later, I was in an Internet café in Covent Garden, not sure of who or where I was, having not slept for what seemed like weeks, and hours after that, in Manhattan, where I'd lived in a former life. My bags had not arrived, and so I was wearing clothes not my own, bought with an airline voucher. Outside, a drill screamed in the harsh summer light—"reconstruction," the Front Desk said—and I tried to push myself down into sleep, somewhere else.

A little after midnight—I was just coming to life and light now—I went out and walked to Times Square, where there was still excitement. A man was cradling his girl's head in his arm, and kissing her, kissing her softly. She stooped down to get into a cab, and he leaned in after her, kissing her again, as if to pull her back.

The cabdriver, with a conspicuous slam, put on his meter, and the car pulled away. A woman nearby was shaking her breasts at a male companion, who looked as if he belonged to another world from hers. He watched her in delight, the screens and lights all around exploding.

The man who had been kissing, kissing his girl, eyes closed, straightened himself up as the car disappeared around a corner, looked around—taxis, crowds, from every direction—and then walked across to a telephone as if to start the night anew. Crowds streamed out of theaters so one could imagine for a moment this was New Year's Eve, the center of the world. The hushed, deserted mosque of the Old City of Damascus—I'd been there yesterday morning—was a universe away.

I walked and walked through the city in the dark, seeing a place I could easily imagine I'd never seen before, let alone lived in for four years. At Sixty-second and Broadway, a man, tall and dark, suddenly raced out into the street, and I stiffened, my New York instinct telling me this was an "incident." But it was just a group of cheerful men from the islands, playing cricket under the scaffolding of a prospective skyscraper at 2:00 a.m.; the man fielded the ball in the middle of the empty road and threw it back as if from a boundary in Port of Spain. Around the all-night grocery stores, the newsstands, people were speaking Hindi, Urdu, who knows what language, and epicene boys were wiggling their hips to catch the attention of taxis.

Elsewhere—last night in Damascus again—people were huddled on stoops, against buildings, bodies laid out as if no longer living, scattered across the steps of shuttered churches. A woman crouched on the steps of an all-night market, three suitcases in front of her. A man reciting to himself, outside a darkened theater. Another wheeling a suitcase across a deserted intersection—2:57, says the digital clock outside the bank.

I'd never seen these signs of poverty, this dispossession, in all the years I'd lived here, but in the dead of night a kind of democracy comes forth. The doorman says hello to me as I pass, and the night manager of a McDonald's laughs at a drunken joke as if he's never heard it before at 3:15 a.m. On the floor of the same McDonald's, a group of kids sits in a tribal circle.

On Sixth Avenue, as I walk, a clutch of Japanese tourists, twenty or thirty of them, following a woman under a flag, stand silently, waiting for the light to change. As soon as it does, they walk across, en masse, as unfathomable as everything else here, off on some kind of night tour.

An all-night guard is saying something about a colleague who got lost. A tall, tall girl with a model's ponytail is hailing a cab on Eighth Avenue. A woman with a shock of blond hair, a leopardskin coat, is traipsing after a man in a suit, while another woman sits up and goes through her worldly possessions: a bundle of blankets beside her on the street.

I could be in Manila again, I suppose, on the night side of the world. Certainly I feel as if I've never seen this place around me, even when I lived here and worked many a night till 4:00 a.m., taking a car back through the deserted streets before awakening and coming back to the office after dawn. When the light comes finally up, and I go to breakfast at a fashionable hotel across from where I'm staying, the friend who greets me tells me that there was an incident last night, a mass murder in an all-night fast-food store. Five bodies discovered in a pool of blood; it was on all the morning news shows.

"That's strange," I say (in Damascus now, Covent Garden?), "I never would have guessed it. I was out in the street last night, walking and walking; the city never looked to me so benign."

2 0 0 2

A
HAUNTED
HOUSE
OF
TREASURES

$\mathcal{E}$yes followed me everywhere I walked around the half-lit monuments of Angkor—out of darkened doorways, out of openings in the carvings of devils and gods, out of little Buddhist shrines illuminated by the flicker of a guttering candle. An old crone waved an incense stick at me as if it were a curse, and another, her lips stained red with betel nut, spat out what looked like blood. Everywhere, soldiers were standing in the shadows of the temple, scarcely discernible by candlelight, and a white-robed soothsayer, in a sudden patch of sunlight, was dealing out futures to villagers. The Buddhas I saw in corners were not serene or reassuring presences, as they might be in other parts of Asia; they were skeletal, often, or pinch-faced, like wraiths in some complex pagan pageant (as befits, perhaps, an area that went from Hindu to Buddhist to Hindu to animist monuments during the six centuries of its creation). All around the scores of temples scattered across seventy-seven square miles of jungle in northwestern Cambodia, there were images of snakes, of leper kings, temples to Yama, God of the Dead.

"Look, there are demons here, look," said my guide as he pointed out the frescoes that twist and swarm across the sprawling complex known as the Bayon.

Indeed, there were demons everywhere. Every time I got out of my car, wild and dusty children swarmed around me, like spirits of the jungle, waving Buddha amulets at me, waving fans and postcards, calling out, "Mister, mister, only one dollar." Their sweet, strange faces seemed spooked, of a piece with the ancient carvings all around, and if I said no to one, her features would scrunch up till they looked like a howl, and her eyes themselves a hiss.

From the trees all around came the chattering of green parrots, and in and out of all the stone corridors of the temple, children were slipping and slithering, parroting back the sad excuses of foreigners with an eerie exactness: "You come back tomorrow, you buy from me?" "You buy T-shirt, you buy only from me? Sir, sir, you buy from me?"

On New Year's Day I drove into the darkness, with a handful of others, a lonely winking light from a policeman on a motorbike in front of us guiding us through the dark. At 4:00 a.m. or so we disembarked near the temple of Preah Khan, a twelfth-century Buddhist monastery almost enfolded in jungle, and, each of us handed an oil lamp, were invited to walk into the night.

We walked and walked, through a long avenue of candles, the forest buzzing on every side, the trickle of lamps in front and behind flickering like fireflies. Into the heart of the old, half-ruined building, up unpaved steps, through a chattering of crickets from the silk and cotton trees nearby. Through a chamber for Buddha, another for animist spirits, a sudden phallic Shiva shrine. Every now and then, by the light of candles placed in the broken windows, we could see a man, watching us in the dark, a child creeping out from behind a pillar.

Finally, after forty-five minutes of walking through the lane of lights, we came into an open space at the far edge of the eastern causeway to see white-cloth tables and all the appurtenances of a sumptuous New Year's Day champagne breakfast laid out in the jungle (put on, free of charge, by the Grand Hotel d'Angkor). And slowly, as the light seeped into the area—a group of Cambodians gathered on a ridge above us, in cowboy hats and baseball caps, and the red-and-white scarves associated with the Khmer Rouge—we watched the features of the ancient structure emerge from out of the trees and come into sharper focus.

Then, suddenly, from a nearby courtyard, we heard the sound of traditional Cambodian instruments. We followed our ears to the Hall of Dancers, where a troupe of tiny children from a local school was performing angel dances in the place erected for such rites eight centuries before.

I had, I suppose, brought an active imagination to Cambodia, and all the associations built up over years of the great extended holocaust of my lifetime, the Khmer Rouge nearby having killed 1.7 million of their countrymen in fields like the ones around here. But still, I had gone there with no particular expectations, simply to accompany my mother to the legendary religious site that she had been dreaming of since she was a little girl.

In the other old monuments of the world—Machu Picchu, Borobudur, the pyramids of the Yucatan and Egypt, Rome—I had been forcibly reminded how insensitive I am to history; they were living places, certainly, charged with the memories of all that had taken place there, but I had left them feeling they were of interest mostly to historians or sightseers.

Angkor, however, was different. It was alive, for one thing, electric with the unburied presences of the jungle all around, the soil, the long-ago workers who had built temples across an area twice the size of Manhattan, and the blood-soaked fields on every side. Angkor was the shrill whine of cicada bells issuing from the trees, and the little girl who put a pink water-pistol in her mouth and pulled the trigger. It was the bullet holes in the temples and the marks left by recent tanks, and the creepers enfolding the shrines of the "holy city" (as "Angkor" truly means), the fingerlike roots swallowing up lichened archways, the protruding branches encircling a face of Vishnu, snakelike vines threatening to pull the buildings back and back into the forest.

At times there is an overpowering sense of Eden to Angkor—the virgin light falling through the trees; the houses on stilts above the green, green paddies; the water buffalo clomping along immemorially beside Tonle Sap lake. But look a little closer, and you notice a one-legged man hobbling towards you with a dirty cup extended, or a swan-necked girl following your every movement from afar. Walk along the main national highway, unpaved a few minutes out of town—a lone cyclist peddling past in the rustic, languid light—and you can feel yourself in some sepia-colored dream of a temple in a jungle from an earlier time. But tugging at you from the edge of the idyll is a girl who stops at the waist, rolling towards you in her aged wheelchair, and pulling you back into something primeval—atavistic—where all the lights are off and you can't tell right from wrong.

One reason I had gone to Angkor now was that, for the first time in my memory, it had become possible to visit the embattled monuments with relative ease. For years I'd been trying to fix up a trip for my mother, but every time I was about to make our reservations, fighting would break out again, or some political convulsion would yank the country back into the darkness, behind the creepers. The area around Angkor is still not entirely safe—2.6 million land mines remain unexcavated there, I was told, and it could take twenty years at least to find them all—and the political situation is still as changeable as the wind. But now, for the first time since 1969, there were direct flights to Siem Reap (the provincial town four miles from Angkor Wat) from Bangkok, allowing you to bypass the tumult of the rest of Cambodia. And, as of the last day of 1997, the Raffles International Group of Singapore had reopened the restored Grand Hotel d'Angkor, a sumptuous French colonial palace built in 1929, and now a luxe homage to the nostalgia of Indochina, all wicker chairs and slowly turning fans and teak paneling, a vision of Banana Republic chic.

Knowing that Angkor had been cut off from the world for more than twenty years, and knowing that it could disappear again at any moment, if not through the intermittent fighting nearby, or the simple encroachments of the jungle, then through the sheer press of human bodies, I told my mother that we should go now. Angkor would never be frictionless, I thought, but it would surely never be much more accessible than now.

· · ·

I think of myself as a relative veteran of all the moral and political conundrums of visiting difficult and wounded countries—in Tibet and Burma and Cuba, I had wandered through every corner of the debate about whether to go to a land in which almost every penny you spend will go towards a government that is oppressing its people and destroying their culture. I'm used to those wrenching forms of calculation whereby one tries to puzzle out how much one is helping those in need with cash and information and visions of a distant world (changing their own home in the process), and how much one is harming them. Yet I've seldom felt the ache so plaintively as in the Grand Hotel, where every $6 cup of tea costs as much as the average Cambodian earns in a month (and the $1,400 a visitor may spend on a bathrobe in one of the elegant boutiques could support a whole village for a year).

Sometimes I stood on the terrace of my beautifully appointed room—all wooden desks and framed prints, with copies of the *Herald Tribune* flown in to the gleaming Business Center every day—and watched the workers far below, crouching down to make the four formal gardens, the jogging track, the twenty thousand trees around the swimming pool and pavilioned spa immaculate. As soon as the hotel walls ended, the overgrowth began again, and there was nothing in the distance but a rusty-looking Ferris wheel.

When you visit Angkor Wat, the glorious centerpiece of the Khmer Empire (so central to the country's sense of itself that it has appeared on five consecutive national flags), you find yourself walking through a long causeway of the crippled: a boy grins at you from a broken wheelchair, a man with stumps for legs holds out his hand for help, others in khaki fatigues like ghosts from the time of Pol Pot smile over their souvenirs, and little girls with cataracts in their eyes play with monkeys on a string.

It is a transporting thing to come upon the vivid carvings of the temple that take you up, up, up, the chambers filled with gods and candles, to a roof from which you can look across the trees (the Buddhas around you sitting under the protective hood of a cobra). Yet it is a desperately poignant thing, too, to see the children, with faces that are unnaturally old (and bodies that seem unnaturally young), calling out, in all the languages of the world, "Hello, papa! *Madame, madame! Esta bella!*"

What I learned by day, then, was supplemented by the lessons of the night. In the blue tropical mornings and afternoons, I took in the wonders of the past; after nightfall, I returned to the hotel, paged through a copy of *The Merchant of Venice* in its paneled library, and mused on all the riddles of the present. To give money to that little girl whose face looked as if it had been deformed by acid might be, inadvertently, to give money to the Khmer Rouge guerrillas who were still shadowing the country; yet to withhold money from her might be to hasten her decline. And why give it to her and not to the man on crutches, or the blind father wailing a plaintive melody? Cambodia is a kind of emotional puzzle with spikes, and anyone who puts his hand into it emerges with bloodied fingers.

The locals I met, of course, seemed to see only good in tourist faces. "Now is a marvellous time for us," said a young friend called Phalla, one lazy afternoon in Siem Reap. "Now we have cell phones; three years ago, only guns. When I came to Siem Reap, ten years ago, we never saw a foreigner." For Phalla, clearly, tourism was a blessing from the heavens, offering him opportunities that had not been known in the Cambodia of his lifetime. He had picked up English (and watched CNN every morning over breakfast in a tiny local café); he dreamed of setting up his own travel agency.

"Tourism is good for us," he went on, echoing the New Year spirit. "We worry about our monuments, the conservation; but we are happy that the money is here, even if only seven percent, eight percent goes to the temples." When Pol Pot instituted his Year Zero in 1975, people were routinely executed for wearing glasses, for speaking English, even for having gone to school; to this day, therefore, Cambodia is even more desperate than its status as the poorest country in the world outside Africa (in per capita terms) suggests. By the time Pol Pot returned to the jungle in 1979, there were scarcely three hundred people in the whole country who had had higher education.

And when I looked at the little girls selling postcards for a dollar a set, I wondered what alternatives they really had. If they weren't living off visitors, how would they be living at all (given that their fields, their lakes, their villages had been devastated)? Tourism was turning the children into parasites, yet the absence of tourism might turn them into skeletons. (It was striking, too, to see how these kids with no formal schooling were picking up bits of Japanese, French, Italian, and English.) Give money officially to Cambodia (as the U.N. had done recently, to the tune of $2 billion), and it promptly disappears inside the coffers of those who need it least; put it into the hands of a child in a T-shirt with a skull on it, and at least it goes to someone who seems to need it.

At the Grand Hotel, the workers in the hallways, achingly sweet and eager to please—every time I passed them in the corridor, they would stop what they were doing to smile, and wish me a good evening—seemed glad of the chance to have any work, and to expand their horizons. Most of them—such is

Cambodia's misery—had learned English only because they had been forced out of their country to refugee camps in Thailand, where English was taught. On New Year's Eve, they placed candles in lotus leaves and sent them floating across the hotel swimming pool, turning the night into a field of little lights.

The people who officially oversee the "City of Monasteries"— "Auctorité Apsara," as the signs on the vans call them—try hard to ensure that tourism does not overrun the mysterious site. So far they have resisted the idea of a sound-and-light show at Angkor Wat lest it damage the sandstone walls, and they try to enforce strict rules over all the new buildings that are coming up (the road from the airport into town is lined with multistory new palaces being built, all hotels, but all constructed, by decree, in traditional Khmer style). Goodwill, however, is powerless against sheer need, especially in a country as broken as Cambodia: when a foreign company comes in and wants to build a hotel larger than four stories, all it needs to do is place a few coins in the right palm, and suddenly the rules are forgotten.

"There are serious, serious problems connected with mass tourism," I heard on New Year's Day from a foreign archaeologist, one of the many overseas workers who are laboring heroically to protect Cambodia's monuments and its people. "But so long as some of the money goes to Cambodians, it does some good. They may get a museum going, they may start returning statues from the Conservation Office stores to the sites." Right now, the fact remains that one of the most astonishing World Heritage Monuments on the planet still lacks a real museum on site, or any kind of visitors' center from which to get reliable information or help.

And so, already, a visit to Angkor Wat at sunset is a journey through a mini–Coney Island of sightseers and tour buses and legless Cambodians trying to make contact with them. Urchins come up to you with postcards, soft drinks, guidebooks. *"Onne-san! Nomimono? Mitte, kudasai!"* ("Sister, you want a drink? Look, please look," in Japanese). A trio of broken men play stringed instruments, and toddlers use the discarded boxes from Kodak film as toys.

"You remember me?" a little girl cries out in the failing light. "I saw you yesterday, Preah Khan. Yesterday you say tomorrow. Sir, you remember me?"

The final complication of Angkor, of course, is that the temples themselves are as vulnerable as the country around them, and the government's very realization that Angkor is its greatest asset has done as much to imperil the monuments as to protect them. Ever since the temples were first built, more than a millennium ago, they have been a prime target for looters, often from abroad (even André Malraux, later France's minister of culture, was apprehended trying to smuggle nearly a ton of statues out of Angkor in 1924), and the chaos and desperation of recent decades have only intensified the pillage. Even now, many-ton statues (hardly easy to transport across borders surreptitiously) suddenly show up in Bangkok antique-rooms, while other price-less antiquities are found in the jungle, broken, a few hundred yards away from where they sat for centuries. As recently as 1993, the Khmer Rouge were holding the exquisite temple of Banteay Sari hostage—close to fifty land mines have since been exca-vated here—and seemed ready to take Siem Reap. And when the guerrillas are not looting the temples for their own gain, the equally penniless military men are doing so, with the help of power drills.

In Preah Khan, the Buddhist training center where I saw in the New Year (another likely target for Khmer Rouge guns in 1993), a British archaeologist, helped by the World Monuments Fund and the Ministry of Culture, has been working for years to restore the site to the state of a "partial ruin" and to train a new generation of Cambodians to appreciate and tend to their heritage. Now, though, the government wishes to cut down some beautiful two-hundred-year-old trees to ensure the safety of the Hall of Dancers, leaving all who care about Cambodia in an agonizing position: to protect the temple is to damage the environment, and yet to do honor to Nature is to imperil Art. And to worry about either can seem almost obscene when forty thousand people in the area are limbless because of land mines, and the children are calling out, "Sir, go to school, go to school. Four hundred, five hundred [riels]."

Besides, what really distinguishes Angkor from most "ancient sites," I was coming to see, slowly, as I wandered among headless Buddhas and children playing weird, thwanging tunes on Jews' harps—the buffet table at the hotel offering "Serpent Head" every day—was that it belongs as much as ever to the haunted countryside all around: to an uncanny degree, the people living around the old temples are living in a way not so different from that of those ancestors who must have erected the buildings centuries ago. You can see a few signs for "Konica Photo Express" in the scrappy little town of Siem Reap, and children can be spotted in weird, batik-y shirts representing Leonardo DiCaprio and Kate Winslet in *Titanic;* but stray only a block from the rickety main street and you are in a village made up, essentially, of crow-

ing cocks and mangy dogs and flimsy houses (one of which collapsed on the mother of a minister while I was there, killing her).
There are almost no road signs or things for road signs to point
to here; when people talk, it is in the age-old terms of fish and
rice and jungle and night.

At the Bayon, a hundred and fifty or so stone faces stare
down at you with the implacable gaze of Easter Island statues,
their expressions not benign or protective, often, but leering,
scowling, grinning with a kind of demented malignity. The place
has always unnerved foreigners (Paul Claudel, the French diplomat and writer, called it "one of the most accursed, the most evil
places that I know," and even Pierre Loti, the lifelong enthusiast,
got "overcome with a peculiar kind of fear" here); but what gives
it its particular resonance now is that the children all around
have faces—wincing, gentle, wizened, sad—that look like
younger versions of the stone ones. It makes you think even
more about their excited talk of the Discovery Channel and the
sticks of incense poking out of 7-Up cans.

My last night in Cambodia I returned to Angkor Wat to see the
magical temple for the final time. Above the long avenue of the
blind, the limbless, and the deformed, a glorious full moon rose,
and a lame man on the ground played a haunting melody on his
flute, as darkness fell and the night began to chatter. The temple
complex was much smaller than I had expected—it does not
open onto a city of other monuments, as I had imagined from
the pictures. Yet the experience of being there was infinitely
more profound than I had expected, and when I went back to the
hotel I knew I would be telling my friends to come to Angkor if
they could—so long as they recall that, together with the eighteen thousand *apsaras,* or attendant angels, that archaeologists

have counted in the area, there are probably an equal number of dark spirits.

The next day, as he took us to the airport, our unfailingly sweet and intelligent guide turned around in the front seat and said, "Thank you for coming here. For giving me employment. Tourists are very important for our economy. Also, for conservation of temple.

"Before, we never thought of this," he said, referring to the protection of Angkor. "If you do not come . . ." With that, his voice trailed off.

In the departure hall, a little bowl had been set up for foreigners to place spare coins or banknotes (worth three cents each), under the sign PLEASE HELP THE POOR VICTIMS.

In the distance, I could almost hear the voices still calling out, "Hello, papa, why you not buy?"

1999

A
NEW
MILLENNIUM

We dropped out of the heavens and looked around us in the dark: a few stone heads; some men in flowered shirts and shorts, handing out leis inside a small, squat terminal; and outside, in the night, a few parking places marked out for the island's governor, its judge, some other dignitaries. Otherwise, there was nothing to be seen in the silence and the dark. Easter Island is the loneliest inhabited settlement in the world, thirteen hundred miles from its nearest neighbor (Pitcairn, population sixty-five), and all around you can feel the miles of loneliness and space. Above us, in the dark, three small white crosses, shining on a hill.

There are not many people who get off the plane at Easter Island, and the few who did all scrambled into a minivan, which bumped and jangled over a brown, unpaved road to take us to our resting places. There are only a few motels on Easter Island—and a few houses made to look like motels—and all of them are next to identical: a patch of grass, some somber stone faces, a bungalow or two around the garden. When we arrived at the one we had picked out from afar, a girl with a long rush of black hair and a white flower behind one ear smiled a greeting but said nothing we could understand. An old man led us to our rooms, and opened the doors on suites so new they came without furniture, without clothes hangers, without anything but space and light. It was dark when I got up the next morning, and when I walked into the lobby the man behind the desk was reading the Bible aloud to himself. He waved his finger mightily in the air as he intoned from the Book of Revelations.

Outside, I could see, as the light began to filter in, there was nothing but grass, running down to black volcanic rocks, the sea. Two thatched huts sat in the middle of the emptiness, looking out on empty space. The only sound I heard, the wind, roaring in my ears.

I needed, insanely, to send a message to my bosses in Rockefeller Center in New York, and so I began walking through the emptiness in search of communications. There are very few vehicles on Easter Island, though there is said to be a bus that runs sometimes on Sundays in the summer. Occasionally a taxi churned past, but then it was gone again, and the place was emptiness and roaring winds once more. And so I continued to walk, down a long, straight, silent road—Polynesia set in Scotland, so it seemed—the silence stretching out on every side of me. There is only one town in Rapa Nui (in resource-poor Easter Island the word stands for the place itself, its language, and its people), and until recently none of the island's three thousand residents was allowed to live outside its narrow limits. There is only one main road in Hanga Roa—the "Navel of the World," as the town is called—and on this particular morning, the world had yet to arrive. A man with long brown hair flowing down his naked back rode past on a chestnut mare. A girl with a sweet-smelling flower in her hair sauntered past as if on her way to Gauguin. Very soon the town was behind me again and I was alone with black straggly rocks once more, a few stone faces and a tumble of old gravestones, white and black and clay-red, tilted against the sea.

I walked and walked, but could find no hint that a world outside Easter Island existed, so I turned back and walked past the tiny park with its tiny pay phone, the little blue café with Tibetan prayer-flags across its courtyard, the shuttered buildings and little souvenir shops. One of these places, selling T-shirts and stuffed animals, offered "Computadores" on its window, but when I looked in, all I could see was a single aged keyboard being clicked away on by a lonely teenager from California. The point of Easter Island, clearly, was to be out of range of the world at large.

I walked down the quiet main street in the early light and came upon a gateway with a life-sized shark at its top. Inside, in a courtyard, I could just make out a sign in blood-red letters that said: E-MAIL. I followed this sign into a little office and found myself inside a travel agency, liberally appointed with books by Heinrich Böll and pictures of the Alps. At a keyboard wild with upside-down question marks and tildes sat a small round man with tufts of white hair above his ears.

"You are looking for a machine?" he said, looking up.

"In a way."

His office was open, Herr Schmid explained, from eight till noon each morning, and then again from four till eight each evening. Often, however, it was closed at these times, too. The clock on his wall, I noted unhappily, recorded "Rapa Nui Time."

I was free to use his machine whenever I wanted, he told me, but I should remember that there were only twenty lines on the island connected to the outside world. Four years ago, the island had not even known direct television.

I walked back down the lonely road towards my motel, reassured in some small way that it was still possible to think of reality in a different light. A few years earlier I had taken to traveling around the New Year, in part because that is the time when our hopes are at their brightest cusp, as, poignantly, is our sense that all the resolutions we're so boldly making will be forgotten by next week. Often, too, I'd taken my mother on trips over the New Year's holidays, to the places she'd been dreaming of since girlhood (Egypt, Jordan, now Rapa Nui). This year the longing to escape the moment was especially intense because the end of the old millennium, as it was being called, was clangorous with millenarian warnings: talk of computers crashing, and plunging us back into the Dark Ages, and terrorists on their way to LAX. On Easter Island, by comparison, a twenty-first-century luxury was said to be a piece of wood.

I looked around me in the silent morning and tried to see where I had ended up. It's a disconcerting thing to fly into the remote Chilean possession from California; traveling west, I had somehow landed up in the same time zone as New York. More profoundly, I felt as if I had landed in the distant past. There was a phone beside each bed in the motel, but just to call my mother in the next room involved connecting with an operator who was never there. A fax machine, it was rumored, sat in the office of the manager, but the manager was never there and the office was always closed. The real wealth of Easter Island is said to be the "living faces," or *moai*, who, the local people believe, travel across the island in the dark to look over their sleeping forms.

I walked towards the black volcanic rocks, the open sea—the "Y2K" that everyone had been chattering about in California the previous day here soothed into something that sounded like "Why today?"—and thought back to Herr Schmid, with his calendars from the Explorers Club showing the peaks of far-off Switzerland. People wonder sometimes why people like him, or Melville, or Stevenson, choose to take themselves away from the comfort of what they know to a place that does not even have a site of higher education. They ask me why I elect to spend much of my time in a Benedictine hermitage—though no Benedictine—or in a two-room flat in rural Japan where I have no car or bicycle or Internet connection or newspapers. When I speak of "infinite riches in a little room" and the twenty thousand sites on the World Wide Web already devoted to information overload, they look more bewildered still.

It's not easy to explain that poverty can take many forms, and that a poverty of horizon can seem as paralyzing as the other kinds. I call that man rich, as Henry James famously said, who can satisfy the requirements of his imagination. Hard to explain, too, that time and space open up as soon as you take leave of the simple ways in which you define yourself. Though many of us are lucky enough not to be afflicted with the actual poverty of which Camus was writing, the longing to live somewhere between that reality and the sun remains potent; luxury, for some of us, is measured by the things we can do without.

Before I came to Easter Island, I knew, as everyone does, that its affluence was measured by the enigmatic statues represented on every poster (and even reproduced outside my local health club in Japan). Yet after I began to walk around the languid

Polynesian island I began to feel that they were the least of the treasures of this forgotten, ever surprising place. Many of them, in any case, had been destroyed years before in tribal fighting and stood now in artificial rows that had no meaning for the people who took them to be ancestral spirits.

Foreigners arrived from every corner of the world and tried to fill the emptiness with explanations. Heroic oarsmen from the shores of South America, or visitors from outer space, they said; Basque influences, perhaps, or what John Dos Passos, at the end of the 1960s, noting the statues' cycle of destruction and rehabilitation, called a "warning to college radicals." For the people who live among them, the power of the statues lies, surely, in the fact that they can't be easily explained; we are as rich as our sense of what lies beyond our comprehension. In practical terms, such inner riches are important; Easter Island is so poor in actual resources that in the nineteenth century people were reduced to eating one another, and the population of the whole place sank almost to one hundred.

Besides, everything around the statues, all the ways in which what thinks of itself as civilization tries to make itself at home in what it thinks of as the wild, was extraordinary. I went one Sunday to a mass at the local church and found a Virgin who greeted me like a staring-eyed *moai*. The Savior by her side looked like another tormented tourist. Altar girls walked through the aisles with collection bags while the priest beamed down on us all, *rongo-rongo* symbols swirling across his white vestments. There had once been an amateur radio operator on the island, Herr Schmid had told me, but he, a priest, had been relocated.

There had once been a woman from Switzerland, too, he said, but then . . . and he said no more.

At the local museum the walls were decorated with decals representing the international credit cards that were accepted, and so I decided to pay for a small purchase with a Visa card. The transaction lasted almost until the new millennium—forty-five minutes in all—and when it was concluded, triumphantly, the young woman behind the cash register raced out, in her delight, and threw her arms around me, planting a wet kiss on my cheek.

I went back to look in on Herr Schmid and found his office closed, its owner wobbling down the main street on an unsteady bicycle. I returned the next day and found a notice on the window saying that the proprietor was away showing petroglyphs to visitors. I went back the next day and found my sometime host being lectured at by a woman from Norfolk, Illinois. He should acquire more modern computers, she said; as it happened, she was in the business of selling these. "If only," said Herr Schmid, trying in his way to explain that, though there was an emergency landing strip for the space shuttle here, FedEx and UPS were not so regular in their visits.

The woman, piqued, replied that she was a member of the Rotary Club, and our host's face picked up with a shy smile. He was, said Herr Schmid, as it happened, the president-elect of the Rapa Nui chapter of the Rotary Club; its members were due to meet this very evening at the Kopakavana restaurant. ("No," he explained patiently, "not the 'Copacabana.'") It was just possible that the father of the current Miss Rapa Nui might be present.

The New Year, the new millennium, drew on, and for a few hours the main street got crowded: a TV crew from Santiago had come to broadcast the New Year here around the world. In the blue Tibetan café with quotes from Neruda across the window, a man in a topknot and tattoos appeared, to speak to the eaves-dropping cameras about how tribal elders had declined, and were hostage, now, to the talking head. On New Year's Eve, when I looked in on him, Herr Schmid confessed that he'd come here for three weeks, eight years ago. On a shelf I saw a little picture frame, and a photo of a beautiful island girl and child.

When at last the twenty-first century arrived, the whole population of the island, as it seemed, gathered on the grassy space in front of the sea, a few stone heads before us. The TV crews put on their lights and some girls sashayed back and forth in grass skirts. Then a few fireworks went up into the sky, so scanty they would have been the disgrace of Norfolk, Illinois, and a great mounting roar of wonder spread around me. For three, four minutes, the heavens were a fountain of pink and emerald lights and the whole island seemed to hold its breath. Then we all went back to our quiet rooms and faced the gusty winds and the empty silence of a new millennium. The messages I'd sent from Easter Island all came with the name "Josef Schmid" at the top.

2000

A

FOREIGNER

AT

HOME

"And this also," said Marlow
suddenly, "has been one of
the dark places of the earth."

—On the Thames, in Conrad's
Heart of Darkness

There is a moment, early on in Kazuo Ishiguro's new novel, *When We Were Orphans*, that cuts to the heart of everything that's odd—to use a favorite Ishiguro word—about this author's not-quite-English fiction. The typically fussy, agonizingly self-conscious narrator, Christopher Banks, never quite sure of his place in the world around him, steps out of a London lunch to pursue a woman to whom he's strongly (if always passively) attracted. When he catches up with her on the street, she starts to reminisce about the careless bus rides she took as a girl with her mother, now dead, and asks Banks if he rides the buses, too.

"'I must confess,'" he replies, in the over-formal English that is an Ishiguro trademark, "'I tend to walk or get a cab. I'm rather afraid of London buses. I'm convinced if I get on one, it'll take me somewhere I don't want to go, and I'll spend the rest of the day trying to find my way back.'"

I can't think of any one of Ishiguro's contemporaries in England who would write in quite that tone of voice, let alone have a protagonist (who's not supposed to be timorous—Banks, after all, is presented to us, without much evidence, as one of the great detectives of his day) confess to such a fear. Yet the response, with all its overlapping anxieties—of dislocation, of losing time, of being swept up in something outside one's control—suggests something distinctive about the Ishiguro world, and something that can still make his maker seem an outsider in the England where he's lived for forty years.

There is a practical reason why Banks might feel ill at ease in London—born to an ultra-British family in Shanghai, he's a relative newcomer in the country of his forebears (and, besides, all his deepest hurts have to do with abandonment). Yet the air of apprehension goes deeper than that. The terror of doing the wrong thing, the elaborate unease attending even the most everyday of activities—take one wrong step and you'll get lost—and the sense of being always on uncertain ground lie at the heart of Ishiguro's poignant and often haunted vision. In his previous novel, *The Unconsoled,* Ishiguro gave us 535 pages about being lost in a foreign place where his narrator couldn't read the signs.

When We Were Orphans may well be Ishiguro's richest and most capacious book so far, in part because it stitches together his almost microscopic examination of self-delusion, as it plays out in lost individuals, with a much larger, often metaphorical look at self-enclosure on a national scale. The story is told in the (slightly priggish) voice, and filtered through the highly fallible eyes and memory, of Banks, a typical Ishiguro protagonist who keeps assuring us how well adjusted and popular he is even as the prose reveals him to be "slightly alarmed" and "somewhat irritated," irked and "somewhat overwrought." Living on the fringes of London society in the early 1930s, in—as he takes pains to tell us—a "tasteful" Victorian house with "snug armchairs" and an "oak bookcase," he longs to have some standing in the world. "My intention," he declares with a typical (and dangerous) mix of innocence and self-satisfaction, "was to combat evil."

More to the point, like all Ishiguro's main characters, he is a foreigner wherever he happens to find himself, homeless even among those snug armchairs: in the Shanghai of his boyhood he is taken to be an Englishman, and in England he is taken to be an odd man out from China. Utterly in the dark, he searches and searches the small print of the world around him for clues as to how to act. (Ishiguro has spoken touchingly of how he, too, arriving in England from Nagasaki at the age of five, learned to "become" an English boy by copying the sounds he heard around him.) And yet, of course, the very deliberation he brings to every transaction ensures that he will never be a part of it. Much as Stevens the butler in Ishiguro's best-known novel, *The Remains of the Day*, laboriously practiced his "bantering" to fit in with the class he served, so Banks, before attending a party, "researched over and over how I would—modestly, but with a certain dignity—outline my ambitions."

It is the foreigner's plight, perhaps, to find himself a detective, as well as an actor, always on the lookout for signs and prompts, and Ishiguro, who is never careless with his details, actually dares to make Banks a would-be Sherlock Holmes (though we have to take much of his success in his profession on trust, since we hear much less about his job than about his advancement in society). Yet the abiding poignancy of Ishiguro's work comes from the fact that his main characters are unsettled in both senses of the word: nervous because they don't belong. The smallest thing (a bus ride, say) can throw them off completely.

The very notion of foreignness has changed, you could say, in the global age (this is one of Ishiguro's implicit themes, and one that would no doubt impress itself on a Japanese writer who can't write in Japanese). The person who looks and sounds like us may (as in Banks's case) be a complete alien; the one who looks quite different from us, and has a funny name to boot, may (as in Ishiguro's case) be so close to us that he sees through all our games. Foreignness has gone underground in our times—become invisible, in a sense—and yet it has never lost its age-old terrors, of being left out or left behind.

In the case of Banks, this suppressed panic comes out in the exile's habit of consoling himself with memories of a place he tells himself is home; however much he is an outsider in England, he can take refuge in the place he lost. Thus, over and over, in his mind, he returns to haunted memories of his boyhood in the International Settlement in Shanghai. One day, seemingly out of the blue, Banks's father (working for a British trading company here disguised as "Morganbrook and Byatt") goes to work, and never returns; a little later, his beloved mother, often recalled laughing in a swing, also vanishes, leaving Banks, at the age of ten, alone in a very foreign country. The boy's one playmate in Shanghai, constantly remembered, is the six-year-old next door, Akira Yamashita, with whom he seems mostly to share a sense of disconnection. "'Christopher. You not enough Englishman,'" says the Japanese boy (in his strange—and to me implausible—English); but Akira, too, returning to Japan, is "mercilessly ostracised for his 'foreignness.'"

Anyone who's read an Ishiguro novel before—and even those who haven't—will feel at home with the sadnesses of a pathetically self-involved character, longing to keep the truth of his loneliness at bay, and training a magnifying glass, in this case quite literally, on the alien world around him: part of Ishiguro's skill is to bring the senses of "pathetically" together (in characters who are moving without always being likable). Yet this relatively precise, and housebound, story breaks into something much bigger when, in 1937, the woman Banks admires (from a distance)—another orphan, called Sarah Hemmings—suddenly goes off with her new husband to Shanghai. Abruptly, and more than a little belatedly, Banks decides that he must go there too—to solve the case of his parents' disappearance, he says (though that happened twenty-five years before), and to bring order, as he somehow believes, to a disintegrating world. When he returns to the lovingly recalled place he thinks of as home, it is, of course, to find it a blacked-out chaos, with Japanese soldiers assaulting the city even as local Communists and the Kuomintang conduct a brutal civil war.

Up to this point, roughly halfway through the book, the reader could be forgiven for thinking he's reading *The Remains of the Day Revisited:* a straightforward (and expert) portrait of a man possessed by truths he can't acknowledge, and missing the boat at every turn (the metaphor becomes an actual event here). Yet as it returns to Shanghai, the narrative acquires a political fury that is not shy of trafficking in the word "evil." Ishiguro has long turned a shrewd and attentive eye—a foreigner's eye, really—on the British specimens he has found himself among, and in *The Remains of the Day* he famously exposed the blind loyalties and vanities of a single butler as a way of pointing up the naiveté of a whole society that invited Nazis to its dinner parties in the 1930s. Here, the assault on perfidious Albion and its "air of refined duplicity" becomes pitiless.

British traders like Banks's father were, of course, deriving much of their income from smuggling Indian opium into China—an activity that had the secondary function of keeping the local populace helplessly sedated. Yet as Banks continues his investigations, he finds that the corruption goes well beyond that: British companies like his father's (which seems to stand in for a well-known trading house still prominent in Hong Kong) were dealing with warlords and, in some cases, sending others off to their deaths in order to protect themselves. And when Banks arrives in war-ravaged Shanghai, it is to find the international elite complaining about chauffeurs and languidly comparing the shells outside to "shooting stars" as they watch Japanese warships turn the city to rubble outside their bathroom window.

Banks is hardly the most assertive of souls, but even he is moved to "a wave of revulsion" by the studied obliviousness:

> During this fortnight I have been here, throughout all my dealings with these citizens, high or low, I have not witnessed—not once—anything that could pass for honest shame. Here, in other words, at the heart of the maelstrom threatening to suck in the whole of the civilised world, is a pathetic conspiracy of denial; a denial of responsibility which has turned in on itself and gone sour, manifesting itself in the sort of pompous defensiveness I have encountered so often.

The point is so alive to him that, fifty-three pages later, he delivers a version of the same tirade, even repeating (a rarity in Ishiguro's perfectionist prose) the phrase about "honest shame." He's so busy haranguing the world around him that he never stops to register that what he's saying applies largely to himself.

And as the novel takes us out of Banks's head, and into the wider world, it also, paradoxically perhaps, rises out of domestic realism to a vivid and often daring surrealism. (At the white-tie gathering under the chandeliers, Banks is actually handed a pair of opera glasses with which to inspect the war outside. "'Most interesting,' he observes, as shells destroy the city. 'Are there many casualties, do you suppose?'") Nearly all of Ishiguro's fiction is set just before or after war, the reverberations of a larger struggle rumbling underneath the action like a distant train; and his great political theme, of nationalism, offers us the shadow side, as it were, of his protagonists' longing to belong. Indeed, the heart of Ishiguro's strength is to bring the two forces into intricate collision, and to show how displaced characters like Banks, precisely because they want to be part of a larger whole, and to serve a cause, attach themselves to the very forces that are tearing the world apart.

Here, as Banks stumbles out into a derelict city of corpses, struggling to find his parents in the midst of all the fighting, it feels almost as if Ishiguro is daring himself to break out of his habitual control and move onto uncharted ground. The writing begins to feel dreamed as much as plotted, and there is an exhilarating sense of its taking on a life of its own and pulling the author into places where he hadn't expected to find himself. (In that small moment on the London street, it's worth noting, Banks finally does get on the bus.)

In the most remarkable scenes in the book, lit up by a sense of outrage and social compassion quite unlike anything Ishiguro has given us before (though he began his professional life working with the homeless), Banks follows a policeman up into a broom cupboard and emerges, essentially, into history. All around him is a wasteland that looks like "some vast, ruined mansion with endless rooms," in his characteristic phrase, and the all but unimaginable suffering and poverty of the "warrens" that the British have taken pains not to see. The very inadequacy of the society detective in the face of real life becomes as harrowing as it is painful: "'Look here . . . All of this'—I gestured at the carnage, of which she seemed completely oblivious—'it's awfully bad luck.'"

This abandoning of solid ground, for writer and character alike, clearly comes with risks. Ishiguro's talk often has to me the feeling of having been as much worked up from research as everything else here ("'Look, old chap, . . . I'm going along tonight to a bash,'" says one character). And as Banks moves through the ruins of the city, more than ever subject to the foreigner's inability to tell friend from foe, or to see the larger picture, some of the dialogue sounds as if it had been mugged up from some black-and-white film about stiff upper lip. "'Now, look here,'" Banks tells a dying Japanese soldier (after attending to his wounds with his trusty magnifying glass), "'I don't want any of that nonsense. You're going to be fit as a fiddle in no time.'" The soldier, whom Banks takes to be his old friend Akira, grunts and, recalling his distant son, says, "'You tell him. I die for country. Tell him, be good to mother. Protect. And build good world.'" Sometimes, here, it is only the Japanese who don't sound Japanese.

Yet for all the occasional awkwardness, the mixing of effects—the poignancy and absurdity of country-house manners brought to people fighting with meat cleavers and spades—turns Ishiguro's gift for blending tones to rending advantage. "Most annoyingly," Banks says, recalling stumbling through the debris with the dying soldier, "my right shoe had split apart, and my foot was badly gashed, causing a searing pain to rise with each step." That mix of "annoyingly" and "searing" says everything that needs be said about Banks: the farce that can break one's heart.

The denouement of Banks's private drama is effected rather too tidily—Ishiguro always has to fight the foreigner's temptation to be overpolite—and the creaking of the stage intensifies when a character we've seen described as an "admirable beacon of rectitude" suddenly tears off his mask to reveal a "haunted old man, consumed with self-hatred." It is everything that is unresolved, mysterious, and in the shadows that gives Ishiguro's writing its power, everything that comes to him strangely, you could say, because he is an outsider. When the bewilderment is cleared up—when the character begins to settle down—the spell begins to fade.

Although *The Remains of the Day* won the Booker Prize and became a huge commercial hit worldwide, Ishiguro himself, always alert with his magnifying glass, referred to the novel as a "wind-up toy"; and as if in response to a book that could be read in only one way, he followed it up with an allegory of estrangement, *The Unconsoled,* so abstract as to be indecipherable even upon rereading. In *When We Were Orphans,* there is a feeling of his having broken through his self-consciousness to activate a passion that was previously submerged; and even as Banks's attempts to keep up appearances—like his wilful blindness— nicely reflect those of the society around him, the book records unsparingly how the larger world's machinations put all his innocence to shame.

The venturing onto foreign terrain leads to occasional melodrama here ("'What you just saw in Chapei,'" a Japanese colonel says, with unlikely fluency, "'it is but a small speck of dust compared to what the world must soon witness!'"); and the tendency to be overpunctilious is not entirely transcended: in the middle of the book, Banks suddenly adopts a ten-year-old Canadian girl, who is so peripheral to what follows that she feels like a narrative device—another orphan, another foreigner, a symbol of the responsibilities Banks neglects and a way of tying pieces of the plot together. Yet this very unevenness can sometimes feel refreshing—and even mark an advance—after the occasionally overworked perfection of books like *The Remains of the Day*.

More important, Ishiguro uses the precedent of the International Settlement as a way of highlighting—and questioning—the very mingling of races that represents the main challenge (and possibility) of our universal Otherness. Salman Rushdie, in his celebrations of the new deracination, looks back to Moorish Spain to show how different cultures can live together in relative harmony; Michael Ondaatje, in his *English Patient*, imagines a desert in which individuals spin around one another like separate planets, no national divisions visible in the sand. Ishiguro, however, on this theme as on most is notably less sanguine than his contemporaries (his father, it's interesting to note, grew up in the International Settlement). National identity is the language and the currency we use, he suggests, and even his Akira and Banks, at the age of six, refer all their triumphs at games to being Japanese or being English (even as they vie to say "old chap" more accurately than one another). In one of the most reverberant moments in the book—as well as the strangest and most typical—the small Banks asks a friend of his parents', "'Uncle Philip, I was just wondering. How do you suppose one might become more English?'" The older man, sounding like many people around us today, replies that "mongrels" like Banks, growing up amidst many cultures, may be lucky enough to exist outside traditional affiliations, and may even bring an end to war. Then, stopping, he corrects himself. "'People need to feel they belong. To a nation, to a race. Otherwise, who knows what might happen? This civilisation of ours, perhaps it'll just collapse. And everything scatter, as you put it.'"

When We Were Orphans traces the collapse of a civilization, and the scattering of just about everything, revealing how the very wish to belong is complicit in that unraveling (and watching the only home Banks has turn into a broken maze of refugees). And in its sadness, as in its willingness to stretch and experiment with realism, it reminds us that Ishiguro is as much a European as an English writer, alien in the deepest way. In many respects, in fact, the novelist he most resembles is that other disciple of Kafka's, living in England for thirty years without ever becoming English, W. G. Sebald. Other than in *The Unconsoled* (the perfect title for all of Sebald's work), Ishiguro has always been concerned with how war affects those not directly involved in it—the theme that Sebald has made his obsession—and how we try to get around all the things we do not want to say (or know). It is a curious coincidence, perhaps, that both writers have been conducting their enquiries into the end of Empire in an England where anti-Japanese and anti-German sentiment run high sixty years after the last war.

When Banks finally comes upon his much-missed family home in Shanghai, it is to find it made over by its new Chinese owners. When Sebald's narrator, in the recently translated *Vertigo*, returns to his hometown in Germany, he can revisit his family's old living room only by checking into a local inn. For both these writers, thrown into motion by the turns of history, foreignness in the modern floating world can only begin at home.

2000

A
FAR-OFF
AFFAIR

"But that was in another country;
and besides, the wench is dead."

—Barabas, in Marlowe's
Jew of Malta

The assault began, really, as soon as I set foot in my parents' India last year. IF AGGRIEVED, said the sign in the Bombay customs hall, PLEASE CONSULT ASSTT. COMMISSIONER CUSTOMS. I wasn't sure that Asstt. Commissioner Customs was very keen to see me, and, besides, I was mostly aggrieved by that extra "t" in "Asstt.," but still I proceeded, head held high, into the merry mayhem. On one side of me was a sign offering a "Liquor Permit," on the other, whatever a "Car Hailer" might be when he's at home. On the far end of the hall, where I went to change my dollars, a sign informed me gravely, PLEASE ENSURE THAT YOUR DRAWERS ARE LOCKED PROPERLY. Looking down to make sure that all was as it should be with my underwear, I stepped out into the gloom, and found myself inside a wheezing knockoff of an ancient Morris Oxford. A "Free Left Turn" was to the right of us, and a "Passenger Alighting Point" to the left. On every other side, the ceaseless Indian anarchy was in full and vocal swing: buses saying SILENCE PLEASE on their sides, the mudguards of trucks responding HORN OK PLEASE, and my own little car making its own small contribution to democracy with a sticker on the back window: "Blow Your Horn / Pay a Fine."

India is the most chattery country in the world, it often seems, and it comes at you in almost two hundred languages, one thousand six hundred and fifty-two dialects, and a million signs that scream from every hoarding, car hailer, and passing shop. But the strangest effect of all, for many a visitor from abroad, is that the signs are just familiar enough to seem completely strange. We passed a "Textorium" as we jangled into town, and a Toilet Complex. We passed the Clip Joint Beauty Clinic, the Tinker Bell Primary School, and Nota Bene "Cleaners of Distinction." One apartment block advised all passersby, NO PARKING FOR OUT SIDERS. IF FOUND GUILTY, ALL TYRES WILL BE DEFLATED WITH EXTREME PREJUDICE.

Feeling more than a little prejudiced myself, I looked around in search of more useful guidance. YOGIC LAUGHTER IS MULTI-DIMENSIONAL, a sign in front of a decaying Dickensian manse announced. Beside it, between some pictures of chunky Technicolor movie stars, a board advised, DARK GLASSES MAKE YOU ATTRACTIVE TO THE POLICE. I could only imagine that they, like most of the notices around me, had been fashioned by some proud graduate of the course I had seen advertised in the national paper, flying in: "We make you big boss in English conversation. Hypnotize people by your highly impressive talks. Exclusive courses for exporters, business tycoons."

In any other country in the world, duly hypnotized and impressed, I would have stopped there: taking note of English misplaced in translation, or imperfectly learned, is not a very useful exercise, especially if you cannot speak any of the almost two hundred local languages yourself. My Hindi, nonexistent, would have provoked more than multi-dimensional yogic laughter. Yet all the miscegenated signs in India speak for something more than just linguistic mangling, and something more poignant: they clutch at you a little with the plaintiveness of a child of a secret union that neither of its parents will acknowledge. A little, in fact, like that sad-eyed man who comes up to you outside your hotel in once British-Indian Aden, and asks you if you'd like to see the English cemetery.

I am entirely Indian myself, by blood, though born in England, and yet I never saw the incongruous merging of those cultures in their prime, or even the protracted divorce that followed upon their falling apart. But even for me, and even fifty years after what is known as "Independence," a large part of the romance of India lies in the culverts and civil list houses, the cantonments and canteens that still dot the hill stations and tropical valleys of the subcontinent. In their day they stood for occupation, even oppression. But now, soothed by history's progress, and standing for a liaison that neither party sought, they speak for something more wistful, to do with the colonizer colonized. And language—the words that startle and bewilder on every side—hints at something that official historians and politicians overlook. As you walk past an "Officers' Mess," across from a sign for the "Bombay Colour Sergeants," you feel yourself in somewhere unique, not quite past and not quite present—the realm of Indlish, or Englian, or whatever you wish to call a curious marriage of inconvenience. (Zee TV in India actually broadcasts its news in what is called "Hindlish.") On my trip across the subcontinent last year I was able, with some effort, to work out what "Free Foot Service" might be (in a temple, no less), and even to deduce what "fingers" stood for, on a menu (a shortened form of "finger chips," or those kind of potatoes the British are always loath to call "French fries"); more than once I found out, the hard way, what it is to have a meeting "preponed" on you. But always I felt that I was speaking a language quite different from the English being spoken all around me (more Indians, of course, speak English than Englishmen), and came to feel that the one companion who'd been with me all my life, the English language, had stolen away into a corner and come back in a turban, a finger to its lips.

The hybrid forms of this unlikely tongue first came into being, it seems, when the merchants and adventurers of the East India Company arrived in India in the seventeenth century, bringing with them their words, their enclaves, and their aversion to all messes not of the officers' kind. Very soon Shakespeare and the Bible were being recited around India. And yet—such is the logic of empires everywhere—the more the seeming invaders held on to India, the more India, somehow, held on to them. By the middle of the nineteenth century, fully twenty-six thousand words had traveled in the opposite direction, from the subcontinent back to England, and many of them referred to goods as indispensable as your *pyjamas* or your *punch*. Deeper than mere words, of course, were all that the words conveyed, as Mother England stocked up on *cashmeres* and *mangoes* and *loot*.

To talk about Empire today is to break very quickly into a contention of "us" against "them." But in its heyday it could never have been the black-and-white affair that polemicists recall (brown, more likely, and shifting, and full of unexpected greys). And today words are how we see the evidence of cultures flirting with one another and mingling and stealing into one another's chambers; the signs of India—CAUSEWAY AND

CROWDED LOCALITY AHEAD or POULTRY CARE CLINIC—are how we see how each was haunted by the other, and how the very sense of rich and poor got challenged and upended. Any Briton who reclined in a sense of superiority over the natives had, in Emily Eden's apt words, the assumption "jungled out" of him, so that soon he was no longer sure whether he was in the light or in the shadows.

As I stepped into an ill-lit office in New Delhi last year, I found myself greeted by a mildewed copy of *Hobson-Jobson*, the great old cobwebbed lexicon of British India that began life as a series of letters and took its name, improbably, from an Englished version of "the wailings of the Mohammedans as they beat their breasts in the procession of Moharram—'Ya Hasan! Ya Hosain!'" And as soon as I opened it up, I was in another realm (more human and more mongrel than in the history books), learning that "ducks" referred to "gentlemen belonging to the Bombay service" and a "Lady Kenny" was a "black ball-shaped syrupy confection." A "James and Mary," I read on, was the name of "a famous sand-bank in the Hoogly River behind Calcutta." The aged book inflected every last sense of "pish-pash" and offered the precise implication of "pootly-nautch." But more than that, it showed how foreignness and its opposite danced so close together that soon it became hard to tell one from the other. "'Home,'" it says, in one of its more poignant definitions, "in Anglo-Indian and colonial speech . . . means England."

For many Britons abroad, no doubt, home came quickly to mean something else, in-between, or nowhere at all: when the Englishman Fowler, in Graham Greene's *Quiet American*, tells a Frenchman that he's going back, the Frenchman says, "Home?" and Fowler says, quickly, "No. England." And in Britain these days the home that many new writers commemorate is some-where on the backstreets of Bombay. *Hobson-Jobson* can tell you the exact social standing designated by a "burra-beebee," it can offer a good definition of "ticky-tock," but it cannot begin to clear up more complex ideas of belonging.

And so simplicities begin to fly out the window, as opium became the largest export of British India and the opium of the masses began flowing in the other direction. These days, I sus-pect, every Englishman worth his salt—every *tycoon* or *pundit* or *thug* (all the words come, of course, from India)—knows what a *guru* and a *mantra* is, and what *yoga* connotes, and has very possibly partaken of them himself. India began by sending its *verandahs* to England, its *bungalows* and *juggernauts*, and very soon was following up with its *avatars*, its notions of *karma* and *nirvana*.

"They gave us the language," says a character in Hanif Kureishi's *The Black Album*, "but it is only we who know how to use it." And though that has the somewhat strident sound of agit-prop, it does remind us of one way in which the conqueror got taken over. Jane Austen has been embangled and set down in the drawing rooms of Calcutta in the work of Vikram Seth, and Dickens has been given a spin and relocated to a dusty Bombay apartment block in the novels of Rohinton Mistry. The Empire never left, it's tempting to conclude; it just settled down in a backstreet in Madras, and started to tell its story from the other side.

To travel through India today, therefore, especially if you are fol-lowing it through its English-language signs, is to see at every turn one culture getting under another's skin, and into its heart and mouth and dreams. And the effect is intensified because the cultures of South Asia seem never to throw anything away, but simply take it all in and stir it up into the mix. You may occasionally be able to make out what is being said to you—DO NOT CROSS VERGE or WATCH FOR SHOOTING STONES—but any resemblance to the language you know is largely coincidental. As I went up into the Himalaya last year, past mouldering Anglican churches whose plaques recalled gallant soldiers killed by a bear (IN THE MIDST OF LIFE WE ARE IN DEATH), I was given instructions at every turn: IF MARRIED DIVORCE TO SPEED or DO NOT NAG WHILE I AM DRIVING. The value of the injunctions was only faintly undone by the fact that I still don't know what many of them mean (NO DUMPING ON BERMS or WATCH FOR OCTEROI).

And even when, by some miracle, you can follow the words, they seem to bite their own tails by being placed in sentences that do everything they can to undermine their own solemnity. Indian English, when it is not overly formal, comes at you with the fatal tinkle of an advertising man who's got his hands on the Ten Commandments: there's always a trace of sententiousness in it, and yet the lofty sentiments are placed inside the jingly singsong of a children's ditty. A decade before, traveling across my stepmotherland, I'd been struck by the signs that said LANE DRIVING IS SANE DRIVING or NO HURRY, NO WORRY, but now they had been joined by half a hundred others, trilling, RECKLESS DRIVERS KILL AND DIE, LEAVING ALL BEHIND TO CRY (or, a little more potently, RISK-TAKER IS ACCIDENT-MAKER). As I drove out of little settlements crammed with such instructions, the signs offered brightly, THANKS FOR INCONVENIENCE. And the majesty of such slogans is only slightly diminished by the fact that five hundred million Indians cannot read a word of any language, let alone the Jinglish commemorated on its roads, and

show no signs of being swayed by LET US SOLICIT THE SEREN-
ITY OF SILENCE (BLOW HORN IF YOU MUST).

It can seem as if a whole new language had been dreamed up
by a clergyman in cahoots with a mischievous schoolboy.
They've drawn their inspiration from Lewis Carroll and pledged
themselves to turn V. S. Naipaul on his head. Never use one word
when thirty will suffice, they seem to say. Never use a simple
locution if a complicated one will serve. Honor your "felicita-
tions" as if you were an "affectee." If you don't blow your horn,
after all, who will?

"The ceremonies should be quite pompous," a friend declared, with sweet innocence, as I stepped into a marriage hall in
Bombay, and I recalled that one memsahib who had never sailed
back to England was Mrs. Malaprop. And when I opened *The
Times of India* ("Invitation price: 2 rupees," it declares, inscrut-
ably, on the cover), I found a whole section devoted to "matri-
monial notices," in which prospective brides were glowingly
described as "homely" and "artful" and "wheat-coloured" (which,
in the crazed logic of Indian English, means domestically
minded, culturally inclined, and fair-skinned). Even at Hare
Krishna Land, the center of the International Society for Krishna
Consciousness, the sign at the entrance extolled its guru's "large
propaganda program" and, inside, in the center's school, a smaller
board offered tips on "Blooming Manners."

You do not have to be much of a polemicist to see, in this
cheerful mingling of proportions, how a country of the poor can
somehow make the playthings of the rich its own, and in that
very act contrive to give the things a gravity and an innocence
they would never have at home. India, of course, is the home of
Sanskrit and of complex philosophies that little in Britain has
ever matched; but what struck me, as I went through some of the
least privileged parts of Bombay, was how the most ramshackle

huts called themselves "Marriage Palaces" and old buses, if they did not style themselves "Stage Carriages," had "Semi-Deluxe" written on their sides, or "Naughty" on their fronts. Even the most broken establishments (especially those, perhaps) call themselves "Honesty" or "Reliable" or "Dreamer's Delight," as if words still had a sympathetic magic here, and just to invoke a quality was to bring its blessing down among us.

When you stumble into a bookshop in Calcutta (the proprietor hands you his business card—"V. L. Chatterjee, B.A., A.B.F.," or "Bachelor of Arts, Appeared but Failed")—you begin to see that the best-selling author of the day is one P. G. Wodehouse, and the faded glory of his diction somehow confers a gay Edwardian tilt on even the most everyday of transactions in India. ("I'm sorry," I was told when I called up the editor of a movie magazine, "Miss Sonaya is not in her cabin just now," which made me imagine her, perhaps not incorrectly, on a cruise ship.) The young these days "air-dash" to what the newspapers typically call a "Mega Exhibition Showcase of Ideal Lifestyle," but everything else proceeds as if nothing had ever changed; as if, in fact, everything is in the hands of some far-off gods who cannot always be relied upon. (The sign that every foreigner comes to know and dread in India, diligently posted up in every airport, train station, and hotel lobby, is INCONVENIENCE IS REGRETTED.) As it says without compunction in a public phone center, ANY EXCHANGE FAULT OR COMMUNICATION ERROR IS ON CUSTOMER'S ACCOUNT. THANKS.

Anyone who is tempted to laugh at all this—as who would not be?—is well advised to recall that in reality the literature of English these days is ever more in the hands of those who may be regretting the inconvenience. They took the words that Empire brought to them, and somehow kept them going, much like those coughing Morris Oxfords in the street, and even made them new. More deeply, they infused the words with a hopeful-ness and sincerity that are elsewhere just a memory. "Devotees are warned," said the sign in Bombay's most famous Hindu temple, "that to sit on the rocks much deep in the sea water away from the sea shore is not only encroachment on government property but is also dangerous to their lives, including valuable ornaments."

We start, perhaps, by laughing at the follies of another cul-ture's misappropriations. We move towards bewilderment, as we sense that we're not quite in the culture we left, and yet not in the one we think we're going to. And we end up somewhere com-pletely different, not quite irony and not quite romance. As I prepared to fly out of New Delhi last year—BE LIKE VENUS: UNARMED, instructed the sign at the airport beside me—I began to wonder how far I was really going. "Blighty," after all, is the Hindi word for "foreign."

1997

THE

PEBBLE

IN

THE

SHOE

Leaving the miraculous out of
life is rather like leaving out the
lavatory or dreams or breakfast.

—Graham Greene

The thing is, the one thing you must never forget," the
Frenchman was saying, calmly, but with a lucid passion behind
him, "this place, it is not Cartesian." The five of us were sitting in
his restaurant in the hills around Pétionville; the suburbs of
Port-au-Prince climb the hills, as in Southern California or the
Côte d'Azur, and from behind the trees, or in one of the lavish
courtyards set against its fairy lights, it's hard to see the contours
of the poorest country in the hemisphere down below. BMWs
purr past and there are swimming pools in the hotels, beside
the villas; at restaurants like the Frenchman's you can dine well
on coq au vin and imagine yourself in one of the finer places
above Nice. A few days later, on New Year's Eve, we would find
ourselves at a $100-a-plate dinner, where all the favored souls

of Haiti, in backless dresses and diaphanous scarves, to show off their tans, would feast as if they were in a boîte in Le Marais. Some were white, many were black, but all were honorary Frenchmen.

The French were perched, though, on the edge of wilderness. In Port-au-Prince itself it is dangerous to go out of the hotels. Men walk around the central square with bloodshot eyes, and it is easy to feel that all of them, at some level, are armed and ready to kill. Haiti is often known as the first country of the Fourth World because it enjoys the rare distinction of having gone backwards since its independence, achieved through the efforts of the released slave Toussaint-Louverture. It is a poetic truth that AIDS was first imagined to come up from this ill-starred island two hours from New York; Haiti's most famous gift is for possessions of the soul, what we call voodoo and zombies (two of the few words it's given to English).

The Frenchman's restaurant was a stylish place, full of nostalgia, and not only *nostalgie de la boue;* lizards ran up and down its walls, and a rat was visible scurrying under one of the outdoor tables, but the man, resident here for twenty-seven years, with a Haitian wife, was doing what he could to push back darkness and claim a little space, a small victory for order. He had realized, however, at what price it came. "It is what you learn here," he was saying, an exile philosopher, over coffee, as the dinner stretched into the early hours. "It is what you must accept. The place is not Cartesian." In Nicaragua, ten years before, during the war, I'd been taken to a restaurant upon arrival where fine lobster was available for sixty dollars a plate (and for dessert to the Café Lennon, where we could play at being Che); the center of the capital was a huge crater still empty from an earthquake many years before.

We were staying now in the Oloffson Hotel, the famous

playground of the international set, where Charles Addams had designed his drawings for the Addams Family, and Graham Greene had set *The Comedians;* one of Greene's ambiguous pieces of local color, Aubelin Jolicoeur, still flitted through the lobby at the cocktail hour, and rooms were named after Anne Bancroft and Noël Coward. The present owner, an exile from America, was the son of a Puritan professor from Yale (and of a Haitian dancer).

He had a band, and we (a schoolfriend and I) followed the band wherever it went; it became our way into the darkness all around. We went with the fifteen musicians to the beach on New Year's Day, a big expedition for local men who lived in the notorious slum known as Cité Soleil. That night we went to a concert held up in the hills, towards Kenscoff; the moon passed in and out of clouds—a voodoo night, as we visitors could imagine it— and at 2:15 a.m. we were the only guests who had shown up so early for the concert. The next day, it was a new nightclub opening on the edge of town, very black men in suits, old men who'd grown fat off various governments, dancing with their wives, while coffee-colored girls in cocktail dresses passed this way and that. We were doing what many in the privileged world seek to do—get a taste of the other side, the place across the mountains, before returning, with sun-browned skins and useful reminders of poverty, to our usual lives.

On arrival—this seemed part of what Haiti was about—a four-piece band greeted my American Airlines flight on the tarmac (the American flight attendants so traumatized that they never stepped off the plane: it was the only place they flew to, a frightened stewardess told me, where they were not allowed to overnight in a hotel). The chaos had begun in the plane itself, the large man next to me pulling out a flask of something potent as soon as we were in the air, while other of his fellows began running hands up any cabin attendants who walked past. (In fact, it had begun even earlier, in JFK, where all the passengers seemed to be carrying all their goods onto the plane with them. I, too, fearing what would happen to my bags if they left my sight, had tried to carry everything onto the plane, and been forced to check in luggage as I boarded.)

Once I walked past the four-piece band into the terminal, I was truly in the wilderness. Thirteen, fourteen baggage carts unloaded their booty onto the belt, people grabbed and pushed, they laughed, my hand, in the melee, began to bleed. But my confiscated case was not in sight. Maybe later, said the harried American Airlines man at the desk; the company could not be responsible for anything. The car taking me into town, once I walked out of the caged terminal (all Haiti, it seemed, gathered in the sun), gave out; the car that would bring me back the next day, in search of my baggage, would get rear-ended, as it stalled on a hill.

The Oloffson was a refuge, of course: its friendly owner had been to prep school in America and the Ivy League; he hardly seemed perturbed when people got possessed at his band's concerts, and started rolling their eyes. Sometimes mobs came into the hotel grounds with flaming torches, wanting to burn the place down; he resisted them almost single-handedly. He did not recommend we go out of the hotel, though, even as far as the Sexy Photocopie shop, or the nearest bar; the bush began outside the hotel gates. It was not Cartesian.

I had a four-room suite (the Lillian Hellman suite, in fact), with a terrace overlooking the garden. There was CNN on the TV, and on the tables were glossy magazines from New York. The magazines, in which I might easily have found an article of mine, spoke of the prosperity and promise of the new Information Age; they spoke of a digital world and man's capacity to get the better of everything around him. The ads were full of jewels and expensive clothes, apt for the pop stars and film directors who stayed here. The people lined up near the Rue des Miracles, outside the Wonderful Semi-Lycée, were relieving themselves in mountains of trash.

It was, I think, the same dialogue the Puritans had known when they arrived in America (and the protagonists of their dramas were two: God and the Wilderness). It was, though the terms would have been different, the dialogue the British entered into when they went to Africa and India. It was a dialogue that takes place inside every being—"redskin" and "paleface," as the literary critics used to say, the genteel tradition and the barbaric yawp—but it was one that it was convenient to describe in terms of Descartes, the round hole and the square peg. The British Empire—or any empire, including the French one here—stands accused of importing straight lines and right angles to a land of curves, of making the forces of Eternity obey a railway timetable. As if one could lay down a perfect grid on a teeming polymorphous swarm (in India, say, in Haiti), which has outlasted all systems and ideologies (and, in India, sometime in its adolescence, had given us, some say, the very symbol we use for zero). It is a dialogue between sense—the forces of progress and order, and understanding—and everything that stands far beyond our apprehension: mystery.

"'I do so hate mysteries,'" says Adele, the young English visitor who has recently arrived in India and been invited to dine with Dr. Aziz, a little before her soul-emptying trip to the Marabar Caves, in *A Passage to India*.

"'We English do,'" says her older, wiser friend, Mrs. Moore.

"'I dislike them not because I'm English but from my own personal point of view,'" she goes on, as a good Forsterian character might.

"'I like mysteries,'" pronounces Mrs. Moore, "'but I rather dislike muddles.'"

A little earlier, the English visitors have trembled to the happier side of the ineffable, as the Brahmin Dr. Godbole suddenly breaks into a haunting, inexplicable Hindu song; it is, perhaps, a large part of what they can cherish in India—the imminence of the unknown. The Marabar Caves round out the equation, though, with the other side of the unsayable, and the comfortable sightseer in the poorer, wilder areas of the globe finds she's in deeper than she knows, in all senses. She can try to rise to the questions mystery raises (as in Melville), but more often she will get swallowed up in them (like the characters in Bowles).

The quester (Adele's last name is Quested) goes out in search of something outside the range of her experience, far from the imprisoning comfort of her life; and she ends up, very often, with some disease, inward or external, from which she will never recover. In the novel in which Adele finds herself, the section called "Caves" is sandwiched between one called "Mosque" and another called "Temple." It is as if some grain of the unknowable, some piece of what is beyond us, gets inside the soul the way a pebble may get inside one's shoe, and after that there is no way of finding the calm one knew before.

The pebble we call mystery, horror, the shadow-world; we call the primitive or the jungle, whatever lies at the very back of us, deep down, in the caves reserved for spirits not of the flesh. The part that comes before cognition, and goes on long after cognition has taken its place on the Cartesian terrace.

My parents (in British India) grew up, I think, in the middle of this dialogue, taught with one part of their beings, the daylight side, to sing of a "green hill far away" and to memorize the verses of Tennyson and Shelley, while with the other they were mumbling ancient prayers, and tying pieces of string around their limbs. Never eating meat or touching a piece of food that anyone else had touched, even if that someone was the one who was teaching them about Locke and Plato and Spinoza.

What was alien to them, in fact, and ravenous, was a world without shadow, where everything was smiling and people had no "side," as the English might have said; the California they came to where there were no Marabar Caves, as such, and yet people wore their lives, their souls, their tremulous destinies upon their sleeves, to be smudged and abraded by everything that passes. To someone who comes from a society of rites, of purdah, it is explicitness, and the elimination of all veils, that can feel unsettling.

This is an obvious point, but it becomes urgent in a world where so many people live in the middle of the Other; each of us is unprotected in different ways, and alienness inheres not in a place or object, but in our relation to it. Our fears—of course— are as private, as unrational as our dreams. For the American Indians, the Puritans were the wilderness, with their figure bleeding on the cross, their hanging of witches from the gallows, their morbid attentiveness to the dark forces all around; for my parents, California was the place where suddenly Plato meant nothing, and Wordsworth didn't scan—all that Britain and India had given them could get no purchase in a world without a sense of history, or center, or direction.

And so they were colonized, in a way, by randomness, the vacuum of a place without society or community, where the old lessons had no meaning; while I, who grew up in the midst of it, had to travel far in search of a more ancestral kind of anarchy and the wild. Which is why, with an old British friend, and a lifelong Christian, I was bouncing now through the wastes of

Haiti, gravestones beside the Route National 1, and shadows stealing through the overgrowth of our hotel to take drinks at the cocktail hour under a folk-art depiction of the Last Supper.

"It's why I read the Bible," my friend said, as we lurched along pockmarked roads till we came to a very old building haunted by pictures of its vanished French occupants, topless in the sun. "Because I fail. Because I'm never the person I would like to be." The town in which we arrived was famous for its murders, and the people were now praying for the next U.S. invasion.

On New Year's Day we went to a small church near the Oloffson, and at the Catholic mass young women in their Sunday best played voodoo drums instead of an organ, and parishioners stood among great pillars on which had been written single words in French: PIETY . . . FORCE . . . FEAR. Something that had existed long before Christ's arrival, and far outside his domain, had come into this building that was itself, I thought, a hopeful, perhaps naive attempt to draw lines around the dark and make a kind of order.

Back in the hotel, on the sunlit terrace, the owner was talking about how he had bought the place for twenty dollars, his partner having left because there were all these people killed in the street. A woman from New York, head of her own P.R. agency, was talking about the time she'd gone out with Warren Beatty, the time she'd met Bob Dylan at Al Kooper's house; when her husband called with a question, she took the call in the hotel manager's office, and her voice rose and cracked as she began tapping her fingers on the desk. The owner's Haitian mother-in-law lay flat out on a bench beside the reception desk as if she were now stuffed.

"Cartesian" was a word I'd never heard in casual conversation before, the Frenchman sipping at his wine, the rats scurrying outside; as we got up in the dark and took the taxi back to the hotel, it didn't really translate to the dark men outside the College René Descartes and the hospital with its sign in two languages, ARMS PROHIBITED INSIDE. At the Oloffson, as the hotel manager and his band played (in the lobby, silent Chaplin films were projected over the painting of the Last Supper), excited fans pulled out their Uzis, and security men sat guard over the fifty or so weapons they'd confiscated that evening. The lines in the maps in my guidebook were all straight and clear; the opening hours were listed for every café.

"I am not seeking an escape from dread," wrote Czeslaw Milosz, after fleeing the shadows of his native Poland for the open spaces of California, "but rather, proof that dread and reverence can exist within us simultaneously." On the streets, the signs said simply, unanswerably, TOMORROW BELONGS TO HAITI.

Thank You

To Lynn Nesbit for representing me so expertly, and Dan Frank for being the guardian of this project; to Robert Silvers, Jim Kelly, Klara Glowczewska, Anne Fadiman, and John Sullivan for being the first sponsors of some of these explorations; to Christine Nolt and Russ Lewin for technical expertise; and to such classic travelers as Jan Morris, Norman Lewis, Peter Matthiessen, and Donald Richie, for inspiring in so many of us the longing to look at the world more closely.

This book is for Louis Greig, the only English gentleman I know mad enough to drop his comfortable job helping to run an investment bank in order to accompany a disheveled schoolfriend to Haiti, Ethiopia, Cambodia, and many of the world's other blighted and transporting places.

A Note About the Author

PICO IYER is the author of several books about cultures converging, including *Video Night in Kathmandu, The Lady and the Monk, The Global Soul,* and, most recently, *Abandon.* His articles appear often in such magazines as *Harper's, Time,* and the *New York Review of Books.*

A Note on the Type

This book was set in a modern adaptation of a type designed by the first William Caslon (1692–1766). The Caslon face, an artistic, easily read type, has enjoyed over two centuries of popularity in our own country. It is of interest to note that the first copies of the Declaration of Independence and the first paper currency distributed to the citizens of the newborn nation were printed in this typeface.

Composed by Stratford Publishing Services, Brattleboro, Vermont
Printed and bound by R. R. Donnelly & Sons, Harrisonburg, Virginia
Designed by Anthea Lingeman